THE GREAT AMERICAN SPEECH

THE GREAT AMERICAN SPEECH

SPEECH

Words and Monuments

STEPHEN FENDER

REAKTION BOOKS

Published by Reaktion Books Ltd
33 Great Sutton Street
London EC1V ODX, UK

www.reaktionbooks.co.uk

First published 2015
Copyright © Stephen Fender 2015

Printed and bound in Great Britain
by TJ International, Padstow, Cornwall

A catalogue record for this book is available from the British Library

ISBN 978 1 78023 521 9

Contents

PART ONE

A Common Culture

O n 14 February 2008, as the contest to become the Democratic Party's presidential nominee heated up into the desperate struggle for delegates from Texas and Ohio, Hillary Clinton sent a special valentine to her opponent. Sensing that Barack Obama's gift for speechmaking was leaving her policy wonkery far behind, she warned workers at the General Motors plant in Lordstown, Ohio, that 'Speeches don't put food on the table. Speeches don't fill up your tank, or fill your prescription, or do anything about that stack of bills that keeps you up at night.' She continued: 'Some people may think words are change. You and I know better. Words are cheap.'[1]

Obama's answer came swift and certain:

Don't tell me words don't matter! 'I have a dream.' Just words. 'We hold these truths to be self-evident, that all men are created equal.' Just words. 'We have nothing to fear but fear itself.' Just words? Just speeches?

'Speeches don't solve all problems', he admitted, 'but what is also true is that if we cannot inspire the country to believe again, then it doesn't matter how many policies and plans we have.'[2]

Though effective as a quick-fire put-down, this riposte also reached well beyond the local political contest. Obama was alluding to words that really did change American history, Great American Speeches uttered by men like Franklin Delano Roosevelt, John Fitzgerald Kennedy and Martin Luther King Jr, a rhetorical tradition of public speaking and writing that runs back through the Declaration of Independence to the first days of settlement in the New World.

More to the point, Obama's allusions to this long tradition were picked up and understood by a mass audience. This is highly significant, because it challenges the recurrent lament of American writers and intellectuals, from Nathaniel Hawthorne, Henry James and T. S. Eliot down to the educational theorist E. D. Hirsch, that Americans lack the historical awareness to place the flux of everyday events into the context of a shared culture.

And while it's true that only a minority of Americans would recognize a quote from Shakespeare or Wordsworth, or even Herman Melville, Mark Twain or Philip Roth, the highly diverse population really does share a culture – not in great literature, or in cathedrals, country houses and traditional social practices, but in public speeches about the values that bind the country together. The Great American Speech *is* the national culture.

The King's Speech

Speeches work differently in British culture, where they are seldom delivered to large crowds in the open air. At times the means of their delivery have taken up as much attention as their content. It never occurred to George V to address the empire until the BBC suggested it. As the likelihood grew that his second son would succeed him, so did the panic about Bertie's stammer. The popular and much awarded film *The King's Speech* (dir. Tom Hooper, 2010) is about how he overcame this handicap to grow into his public role as George VI.

The medium is so important because, though British history can claim a share of great election addresses to large crowds, most of the country's best remembered speeches have occurred indoors, in places to which few, if any, members of the public were allowed access: Lord Mayors' banquets, party conferences – above all, parliament.

In the nineteenth century the momentous words were conveyed to the public through verbatim newspaper reports, often with helpful guides to the audience's response: '(applause)', '(hearty laughter)'. Most of Churchill's great wartime speeches were first delivered in the House of Commons; the people got to know them only through the newspapers or when he re-read them on the BBC. More recently television has relayed the big set speeches given at party gatherings, like Margaret Thatcher's 'You turn if you want to. The lady's not for turning' (Brighton, 1980) and Neil Kinnock's attack on Derek Hatton and his Liverpool councillors of the Militant Tendency, 'the grotesque chaos of a Labour council – a *Labour* council – hiring taxis to scuttle round a city handing out redundancy notices to its own workers' (Bournemouth, 1985).

Memory and Rhetoric

Sound bites like these are how the British remember speeches – not always fondly. Others include Harold Wilson's 'white heat of the technological revolution' (Scarborough, 1963) and Enoch Powell's 'the Tiber foaming with much blood' (West Midlands Area Conservative Political Centre, 1968). But how many can now remember the rest of these speeches, or even their contexts? For that matter who can recall the particular policy on which Mrs Thatcher was refusing to make a u-turn?

In Britain – England in particular – rhetoric and stage-managing are considered suspect. Kinnock was called a 'Welsh windbag'. Great attention has been paid to how Margaret Thatcher trained her voice to sound at a lower register to give it more authority. Even Churchill came in for criticism from his contemporaries. After the Conservative Party elected him party leader in 1940, one Tory MP commented that he was 'a word-spinner, a second-rate rhetorician'. His most famous speech, the one on 19 June 1940 that ended 'People will say, "This was their finest hour"', was thought to be an indifferent performance in the House of Commons, and when he repeated it that night on the BBC, Cecil King, owner of the *Daily Mirror*, thought he must be either ill or drunk.

Reviewing a recent book on Churchill's speeches (Richard Toye's *The Roar of the Lion*),[3] the historian David

Reynolds points out that the great man's rhetoric was often received with 'an undercurrent of criticism about his ego, showmanship and propensity to talk – even after his biggest rhetorical hits'. The people trusted Churchill when he told them the truth, Reynolds writes, even if the news was bad, not when he tried to gloss over bad things, like the German warships' escape from Brest up the English Channel in February 1942.[4]

Americans, on the other hand, accept the rhetoric of public speaking as part of the form. And they often remember great speeches as a whole rather than in sound bites, because they have had to memorize them at school as a patriotic lesson in American national identity.

Topics

In their long history of parliamentary debate the British have encompassed a wide variety of topics. Some of their best remembered speeches have focused on constitutional issues: Charles I on trial for treason in 1649, claiming that a king 'cannot be tried by any superior jurisdiction on earth'; Prime Minister Benjamin Disraeli (1872) on the role of the monarch and the House of Lords; Labour Party leader Michael Foot opposing piecemeal reform of the House of Lords in 1969. Others have argued for reform, from John Wilkes pleading for a wider franchise to include the new industrial towns in 1776 and William Wilberforce proposing the abolition of the slave trade in 1789, to Prime Minister Harold Macmillan in Cape Town recognizing that a 'wind of change is blowing through this continent'. Vows to defend the realm, too, have stirred the emotions, from Elizabeth I's at Tilbury in 1588 to confront the Spanish Armada with 'the heart and Stomach of a King', to Churchill's that 'we shall fight them on the beaches, we shall fight them on the landing grounds, we shall fight in the fields and in the streets, we shall fight in the hills, we shall never surrender'.

By contrast the canonical American speeches are about America itself – particularly on how it might be better than it is. And here is the unexpected thing, when you consider that the overriding American ideology is supposed to be all about free enterprise and every man for himself: in the Great American Speech 'better' has meant more communitarian, more sharing, more tolerant, not more competitive, richer or more prosperous. Gordon Gekko's 'Greed is Good' speech in *Wall Street* (dir. Oliver Stone, 1987) to the shareholders of Teldar Paper shocks and amuses the film audience by how it inverts the usual pieties.

Monumental Occasions

Recent research has shown that Great American Speeches, like elegies and inauguration addresses, often fall far short of their intended effect, whether on Congress or the people. Yet they are revered as national monuments – indeed they often become physically part of national monuments, like the excerpts from Franklin Roosevelt's 1932 accept-ance speech promising 'a new deal for the American people' in the Roosevelt Memorial, and the Gettysburg Address on the wall behind the big statue in the Lincoln Memorial, itself the site of Martin Luther King Jr's 'I have a dream', delivered to the vast crowd in the mall at the rally for jobs and freedom in 1963.

By 2011 King had his own monument, of course, on the southwest corner of the Tidal Basin of the National Mall, near the Roosevelt Memorial, on a sightline between the Jefferson and Lincoln memorials. The great man stands 30 ft high, with his arms folded, emerging in high relief from a rough-hewn granite block. Behind him are two further granite forms, through which the visitor has to pass to get to the figure of King himself. The concept is based on a phrase in his 'I have a dream speech' given before the 1963 march on Washington: 'Out of a mountain of despair, a stone of hope.' A long inscription includes fourteen excerpts from King's sermons and other speeches.

The British don't do this with their memorials, though they have put a poem – Wordsworth's 'Composed upon Westminster Bridge, September 3, 1802' – on the entrance to the London Eye. The contrast is revealing: instead of being directed didactically to the country's loftier ideals, the visitor is invited to consider this new view of London in the historical context of an earlier perspective.

Competing Ideologies

This is what makes the moral orientation of the Great American Speech so unexpected: that it runs directly counter to the 'American Dream', that promise held out to the world's poor and downtrodden that if they were willing to risk the disruptive move to America, work hard when they got there, save their money and put off satisfying their immediate whims, they could become as rich and successful in the New World as their former masters in the Old.

Over time this promise hardened into a set of values to be prized above all other human qualities. The virtues of self-reliance, individual risk, private enterprise, energized by relative freedom from government control, grew into the chief constituents of American national self-identity. This is what historians and populists alike have called the American Dream.

Yet fewer have noticed that all this time Americans have also identified in themselves another, quite opposite, set of ideals, going just as far back into the country's past as the dream of personal success. According to this tradition, the principles distinguishing the nation from the rest of the world are community and equality, in spite of social and economic status.

More often spoken than written – that is, personally presented live and tested by the responses of a live audience – this opposing claim on American identity has always held mass appeal. In popular culture, from sermons and speeches (whether for presidential inaugurations, or just to celebrate the nation), right down to present-day films, the Great American Speech has functioned as a correcting focus on communal themes and values.

I

Immigrants and the American Dream

EARLY EXPLORERS and settlers carried opposing ideals to America. Puritans like Robert Cushman and John Winthrop wanted a sharing society, while adventurers like Captain John Smith thought the settler could be set free from Old World social and economic constraints in order to better himself in the New.

Though the Puritans may have considered Smith's ambition to be the selfish default position of fallen mankind, it was a competing ideology, in its way as radical as the proposition that America should form itself into a communitarian polity. In fact, the impulse for self-improvement had been there from the beginning: a fully articulated programme of its own, part of the argument for 'western planting', as they called the settlement of the Americas, and it was tightly woven into the proposal for American settlement from the beginning.

This argument was advanced, not in stirring speeches but in vigorous prose, both visionary and concrete in its command of the English vernacular. Smith was the resourceful, energetic and courageous leader of the Virginia Colony at Jamestown, from 1608 the first permanent English settlement in North America. While

exploring the Chickahominy River and trading with
the natives for food, as he was later to tell the story in
*The Generall Historie of Virginia, New-England, and the
Summer Isles* (1624), Smith was captured, sentenced to
death and saved only at the last minute by Pocahontas,
daughter of the Algonquin Chief, Powhatan. Smith's
negotiations with the natives and Pocahontas's supposed
love for him, with its figurative marriage of Native and
European, conquered and conqueror, nature and culture,
became one of the founding myths of America.

After being wounded by a gunpowder explosion,
Smith sailed home for England in October 1609.
It was to be some time before he was active again in
transatlantic affairs, but in 1614 he sailed to what he was
the first to name New England, mapping the coastline
and exploring the interior for marketable raw materials.

Like Richard Hakluyt the Younger and those whose
accounts Hakluyt collected in *The Principall Navigations,
Voiages, and Discoveries of the English Nation* (1589),
Smith would become a great propagandist for the western
planting. They wanted to extend English military power,
commerce and reformed Christianity to counterbalance
the Catholic settlements already established by the Spanish
in the New World. They wanted raw materials for home
manufactures. Some even wanted a dumping ground for
the increasing number of vagabonds displaced by the
enclosures of common lands begun in the sixteenth
century.[1]

Smith shared these motives, especially the emphasis
on raw materials. His *A Description of New England* (1616)
contains ample catalogues of New World minerals to be

extracted and trees to be cut down, as well as of animals of air, sea and land to be caught for food to nourish the early settlers before they could plant their crops:

> Oke is the chiefe wood; of which there is great difference in regard of the soyle where it groweth; firre, pyne, walnut, chesnut, birch, ash, elme, cypresse, ceder . . . Eagles, Gripes [vultures], diverse sorts of Hawkes, Cranes, Geese . . . Meawes, Guls, Turkies, Dive-doppers [dabchicks], and many other sorts, whose names I knowe not. Whales, Grampus, Porkpisces [porpoises], Turbut, Sturgion, Cod, Hake, Haddock . . . Oysters, and diverse others etc.
>
> Moos, a beast bigger than a Stagge, deere, red and Fallow, Bevers, Wolves, Foxes . . . and diverse sorts . . . whose names I know not.

The natural bounty of the New World rendered the cultural forms of conventional syntax redundant. It also outran his Old-World taxonomy.

But Smith's ambitions went beyond concerns for material gain, into the future economic, social and even moral progress:

> Who can desire more content, that hath small meanes, or but only his merit to advance his fortune than to tread and plant that ground hee hath purchased by the hazard of his life? If he have but the taste of virtue and magnaminitie, what to such a minde can bee more pleasant, than planting and building a foundation for his Posteritie, gotte from the rude earth by Gods

blessing and his owne industrie, without prejudice
to any?[2]

In other words, those trapped by poverty and low social
status in the bad Old World could prosper in the New.
So long as they had the spirit ('magnaminitie' means a
noble ambition), were ready to take the risk, work hard,
stick to it and (Smith didn't say) had the good luck and
good health to see their project through, they could found
a 'posterity' every bit as substantial and long lasting as the
aristocratic dynasties of Europe.

This was the 'American Dream'. Literally thousands
of such promoters – some disinterested, others with
American real estate to sell – would repeat these
exhortations, and many migrants, as their letters home
made clear, would come to internalize that promise.[3]

Many of these later accounts would repeat the
explorers' catalogues of the New World's natural
bounty, if only in a humdrum list of cheap commodities
available in profusion. William Cobbett, the radical
reformer now better remembered for his *Rural Rides*
(1822–6), had at first been sceptical of the 'trans-
alleganian romance' of American settlement, but by
1817, when he was forced to flee to the United States to
escape the Power of Imprisonment Act of 1817, he had
changed his mind. His book of that experience, *A Year's
Residence in the United States of America* (1828), enthused
over the easy availability of 'tea, sugar, coffee, spices,
chocolate'.[4]

Unlike Cobbett, Morris Birkbeck, son of a prominent
Quaker minister in Guilford, Surrey, had invested in

American land; so he was promoting emigration to the United States out of self-interest as well as political progressivism. His *Notes on a Journey in America . . . to the Territory of Illinois* (1817), which ran through five editions in two years, followed the rhetoric of the catalogue by listing the American prices of meat, poultry and vegetables in elaborate tables. But he was also interested in social observations, commenting for example on the erosions of class distinctions in democratic America – specifically the lack of a servant class (and mentality). 'To be easy and comfortable here', he wrote, 'a man should know how to wait upon himself.'[5] Cobbett too, noted that an American servant 'will not wear a *livery*, any more than he will wear a halter round his neck'. In America even the paupers were respectable:

> A pauper in England is fed upon bones, garbage, refuse meat, and *substitutes* for bread. A pauper here expects, and has, as much flesh, fish, and bread and cake as he can devour . . . An American beggar walks up to you as boldly as if his pockets were crammed with money, and . . . very civilly asks you, *if you can* HELP *him to a quarter of a dollar.* He mostly states the precise sum; and never sinks below silver.[6]

What of the amateur authors, the ordinary migrants writing home to their families left in England? They followed in the same rhetorical footsteps of the professionals. As early as 1632 the Puritan minister Thomas Welde was writing to his former parishioners back home in Tarling, Essex, to celebrate the socially levelling effect of the Massachusetts natural bounty. 'Blessed be God', he wrote, 'here is plenty of corne that the poorest have enough. Corne is here at 5/6d a bushel. In truth you can not imagine what comfortable diet the Indian corn doth make and what pleasand [*sic*] and wholesome food it makes.'[7]

Exactly two centuries later recent migrants were still citing catalogues of natural bounty to express their sense of material progress and general well-being in the New World. Here are Thomas and Jane Morris writing to his father from Washington County, Ohio, early in 1832:

> We have cleared a little land. We raised about 100 bushels of corn and about 40 bushels of potatoes and about 8 bushels of cucumbers and about 10 bushels of pumpkins besides beans, peas, turnips &c. last year and I erned 21 bushels of wheat with mowing & reaping, &c. at 10 bushels per day. We have 2 cows, 2 bull calves, which I intend to have for a yoak of oxen if the[y] have luck, 2 sheep and 24 hogs and 3 we have killed for our winter and spring meat and 13 head of poultry and a dog and cat.[8]

For those who were not growers, the price of food represented equally exciting catalogues of plenty. 'I will tell you the price of goods', John Harden wrote to his parents from New York State in 1828. 'Wheat 5*s* per bushel; all other grain 4*s* per bushel; beef and mutton 2 or 3 cents per pound; veal 3 cents; pork 8 cents; sugar 10 to 12 cents; tea 73 cents per pound; spirits 3*s*, 6*d*. per gallon.'[9]

Away from the market, out in the country, game was equally plentiful. As Edward Phillips wrote from Greenville, Illinois, to his father back in Shropshire in 1842:

> [There are a] great many Deere and turkeys in the country. Any man may shoot if he pleases, and plenty of smaller game, such as rabits, squirrals, partriges, prairie chickens, a fowl something less than the common dunghill fowl, and equally as good.[10]

'Any man may shoot if he pleases.' If you tried that on a landed estate in Old England you could be indicted under the Night Poaching Act of 1821 and transported to Tasmania.

Again and again there is a political message in these letters home, sometimes hidden, sometimes overt. Along with plenty came liberty, as John Burgess, now settled in Westchester County, New York, wrote in 1794 to Thomas Hallett, one of his old friends in Ditchling, Sussex:

> When I lived in Ditchling . . . I know and God knows that I did all that lay in my Power to live, & to live decent but it was all in vain . . . It was Necessity that generated a will in one to take so great a flight, & most happy flight it has been, for hear I am landed safe in a Land of Liberty and Plenty, where a Man by industry, may provide for himself & family, without any fear of having his dear Children taken away from him, & put in a Workhouse to be made Slaves to the Avarice of parish Office Fatgut Farmers, Butchers & Publicans.[11]

In other words, these appeals to emigration were often buttressed by a satire of the mother country that the migrants were being encouraged to leave behind. In *Notes on a Journey* (1817) Birkbeck summarizes the near-medieval situation of a tenant farmer before the Reform Acts:

> An English farmer, to which class I had the honour to belong, is in posession of the same rights and privileges with the *Velleins* of old time, and exhibits for the most part, a suitable political character. He has no voice in the appointment of the legislature unless he happen to possess a freehold of forty shillings a year, and he is then expected to vote in the interest of his landlord; he has no concern with public affairs excepting as a tax payer, a parish officer, or a militia man. He has no right to appear at a county meeting, unless the word *inhabitant* should find its way into the sheriff's invitation; in this case he may show his face among the nobility, clergy, and freeholders: – a felicity which once occurred to myself, when the inhabitants of Surrey were invited to assist the gentry in crying down the Income Tax.[12]

As for taxes in America, wrote Cobbett:

> there is no *excise* here; no *property* tax; no *assessed* taxes . . . No window peepers. No spies to keep a look-out as to our carriages, horses and dogs . . . But then we have not the honour of being covered over with the dust, kicked up by horses and raised by the

carriage-wheels of such men as Old George Rose,
. . . [who has] pocketted more than *three hundred
thousand pounds* of the public, that is to say, the
people's money. There are no such men here.[13]

Because of the ultra-conservative nature of the English
social and economic structure, Cobbett argued, there
would be no point in prospective emigrants uprooting
themselves only to go to one of the English colonies
overseas – say, Australia. 'We read the other day', he
warned, 'of the execution of *nine culprits at once* in
the happy colony of New South Wales . . . and that the
governor had, *by proclamation*, just increased the *duties*
on tobacco and spirits.'[14]

It was John Smith, though, who had provided the
definitive satire on Old World living. Using the full range
of English rhetoric and diction (including slang, like
'sharke' for 'sponge') that might almost be Shakespeare
writing in prose, he produced the most coruscating
imaginable denunciation of staying at home:

Then who would live at home idly . . . onely to eate,
drink, and sleepe, and so die? Or by consuming that
carelessly, his friends got worthily? Or by using that
miserably that maintained vertue honestly? Or, for
being descended nobly, pine with the vaine vaunt of
great kindred, in penurie? Or (to maintaine a silly
show of bravery) toyle out thy heart, soule, and
time basely, by shifts, tricks, cards and dice? Or by
relating newes of others actions, sharke here or there
for a dinner or supper; deceive thy friends by faire

promises and dissimulation, in borrowing where
thou never intendest to pay; offend the lawes, surfeit
with excesse, burthen thy Country, abuse thy selfe,
despaire in want, and then couzen thy kindred, yea
even thine owne brother, and wish thy parents death
. . . to have their estates.[15]

In contrast to the critiques of the radical Cobbett or
Birkbeck the speculator in New World real estate,
Smith's denunciation, rather than taking sides in a
contemporary political debate over duties or the franchise,
is more personal and at the same time more comprehensive: the discrediting of a whole way of life that might be
described as not only metropolitan but urban. You need
to move to America, he is saying, to save yourself from the
enervating corruptions of the big city. He focuses not on a
political party but on the individual enterprise of self-help,
of personal reformation.

In other words, Smith wanted to persuade prospective
migrants to settle in America, not because they would
move to a more socially and economically progressive
society – in any case, in 1616 the only social organization
in New England was that of the Native Americans – but
because their escape from the social, economic and even
moral confines of the Old World would free them to use
their own talents and strengths, hard work and courage,
to work out their own salvation.

Whether or not tied to a specific political programme,
these persuasions to emigrate were radical, inspiring and
progressive in their effect. Radical because those who took
up the challenge would be leaving behind friends and at

least some family, possibly a familiar occupation or other work, even whole cultures. Inspiring because they caught the imaginations, and in many cases informed the behaviour, of countless ordinary people. And progressive because they offered a chance to improve economic and social position to many caught in Old World hierarchies of class and ownership.

2
'City on a Hill':
The Communitarian Vision

THE FIRST GREAT AMERICAN speeches proclaimed and justified the English settlement of New England. In the early summer of 1630, the English Puritans sailed westwards on the *Arbella*, the flagship of a twelve-strong fleet on its maiden voyage to the New World. One of their leading figures was John Winthrop, an English lawyer who was later to become governor of the Massachusetts Bay Colony. En route he penned a sermon which he delivered after reaching the other side.

Called 'A Model of Christian Charity', the speech enjoined his fellow settlers to work together, sharing their fortunes both good and bad, in order to make their new colony a model of its kind, a Christian improvement on the more secular commercial and imperial ventures being set up elsewhere in the New World. To our greatest 'praise and glory', he argued, 'men shall say of succeeding plantations, "The Lord make it like that of New England." For we must consider that we shall be as a city on a hill. The eyes of all people are upon us.'

Winthrop's address has gone down as one of the sacred texts of American identity, reproduced – though often only in part – in countless anthologies of American literature, and quoted in both popular and learned works of cultural and political history as a pledge to make America the exception to other nations. It has even been taken as a prophecy of later historical developments like American independence and the country's mission to convert the rest of the world to democracy.

Typical of the almost scriptural awe in which historians have enshrined Winthrop's words is the Exodus-like first page of the historian Gabor S. Boritt's *Lincoln and the Economics of the American Dream*:

In the beginning were the land and the dream. The Land, Robert Frost has written, was 'vaguely realizing westward, but still unstoried, artless, unenhanced'. The dream was as old as mankind, of the 'city upon a hill', a light to the world, where men were endowed with the right to rise in life.[1]

Winthrop did want his new world of Massachusetts to be exceptional – the propagandists for the American exception got that right – but not in endowing men 'with the right to rise in life'. Exactly the opposite, in fact. What Winthrop argued was that the desire 'to rise in life' was part of the original sin, the result of mankind's Fall.

The reason why so many apologists for American exceptionalism have misunderstood 'A Model of Christian Charity' is not just that they haven't read it carefully, but that they don't recognize its context, the Great American Speech. And the very first Great American Speech was given nine years before Winthrop's Massachusetts Bay Colony set sail from England. It was called 'The Sin and Danger of Self Love', and along with its author, Robert Cushman, it has since sunk into a deep – and deeply undeserved – obscurity, despite the fact that it was spoken to the legendary 'Pilgrim Fathers', those other Massachusetts Puritans, who settled in the Plymouth Colony.

Unlike the Massachusetts Bay settlers, those at Plymouth were separatists. Rather than remaining in communion with the reformed Church of England, hoping to reform it further from within, they had broken with it altogether. As such, they were less connected to the establishment, less well funded, less well educated and less numerous than their soon-to-be neighbours in Boston. Cushman was their backroom boy. He negotiated a patent for the new colony and managed its funding with a London joint-stock company. He arranged the lease of the *Mayflower*, the ship that would carry the settlers over to Cape Cod, then later to Plymouth, Massachusetts.

Though he set sail with the Plymouth Separatists, Cushman had to turn back when his ship sprang a serious leak. He didn't arrive in New England for almost a year after the first settlement. By then a few issues had developed between the Pilgrims and the merchant adventurers back in London. The settlers still hadn't signed the ten articles of agreement between them and their backers. They had kept the *Mayflower* with them longer than required, then sent it home empty, without so much as a load of timber to defer some of the investors' costs. They were also beginning to chafe at the company policy that they should share the new land. Some wanted it divided into private parcels and distributed among them.

So Cushman's first task was to convey how strongly the merchant adventurers felt about their signing the articles and remitting some raw materials to England – so strongly that they threatened to withhold all future backing if these conditions were not met. So the colonists signed. Then they loaded up the *Fortune*, the ship in which Cushman had arrived, with timber and furs traded with the natives.

As for sharing, Cushman considered it to be not just company policy but a matter of Christian conscience. On this topic, although he was a deacon only and not a fully fledged minister, he judged he would need to deliver a sermon. And so, on 9 December 1621, the first anniversary Sunday of the Pilgrims' landing in Plymouth, Robert Cushman gave the first ever Great American Speech.

'The Sin and Danger of Self Love' began, as Winthrop's 'A Model of Christian Charity' would later end, by comparing the devout settlement in Massachusetts with other English colonies in the New World. The infant colony in Virginia, established in 1607, had been motivated by self-love, Cushman thought. Though the Virginia settlers were courageous in removing themselves 'out of a thronged place into a wide wilderness', yet many did so 'out of discontentment in regard of their estates in England; and aiming at great matters here, affecting to be gentlemen, landed men, or hoping for office, place, dignity, or fleshy liberty'.

Taking his text from Paul's first letter to the Corinthians (10:24): 'Let no man seek his own: but every man another's wealth', Cushman warned his audience that 'The vain and corrupt heart of man' is like 'a belly-god, host or innkeeper' who welcomes his guests 'with smilings, and salutations, and a thousand welcomes', but if the bill goes unpaid, 'his smiles turn into frowns, and the door set open, and their absence craved'.

But just what is self-love? Cushman gives five varieties, three of which are salient. The first, 'seeking riches, wealth, money', gets in the way of all other priorities. The second is seeking 'ease or pleasure'. 'Such idle drones are intolerable in a commonwealth', he added pointedly. The last is wilfulness. 'Some men are so prince-like, or rather Papal, that their very will and word is become law, and if they have said it, it must be so, else there is no rest or quietness to be had.'

What are the causes of self-love? Pride, of course, conceit, lack of consideration for others, even a general failure to value 'other men's endowments, abilities and deserts'. And 'wealth' means more than just 'riches'; it also takes in other benefits, like 'comforts, either for soul or body', and 'favours' done or shown.

These lessons applied especially to Plymouth, because as a spiritual 'league and covenant in the Gospel', the community was made up of members of one body. For some to look out for themselves and ignore the others would be as absurd 'as if a man should clothe one arm or one leg of his body with gold and purple, and let the rest of the members go naked'.

So what follows from the obligation 'to cleave together in the service of God and the King'?

May you live as retired hermits? and look after no body? Nay, you must seek still the wealth of one another; and enquire as David, how liveth such a man? How is he clad? How is he fed? He is my brother, my associate; we ventured our lives together here, and had a hard brunt of it and we are in league together. Is his labour harder than mine? Surely I will ease him; hath he no bed to lie on? Why, I have two, I'll lend him one; hath he no apparel? Why, I have two suits, I'll give him one of them; eats he course fare, bread and water, and I have better, why, surely we will part stakes. He is as good a man as I, and we are bound each to other, so that his wants must be my wants, his sorrows my sorrows, his sickness my sickness, and his welfare my welfare, for I am as he is. And such a sweet sympathy were excellent, comfortable, yea heavenly, and is the only maker and conserver of churches and common-wealths, and where this is wanting, ruin comes on quickly, as it did here in Corinth.

Cushman's message was stark: Plymouth could either fail through private enterprise or thrive as a 'common-wealth' (to this day Massachusetts is a 'commonwealth', not a 'republic', as Texas and Vermont used to be, or a 'state' like most of the rest). And common wealth would have a practical bearing on the community's development too, since

It wonderfully encourageth men in their duties, when they see the burthen equally borne; but when some withdraw themselves and retire to their own particular ease, pleasure, or profit, what heart can men have to go on in their business? . . . Great matters have been brought to pass where men have cheerfully as with one heart, hand, and shoulder, gone about it, both in wars, buildings, and plantations, but where every man seeks himself, all cometh to nothing.

It is too early in the settlement for private enterprise, which in any case is made to look shabby by its association with luxury and greed.

Paul saith, that men in the last days shall be lovers of themselves (2 Tim., 3:2) but it is here yet but the first days, and (as it were) the dawning of this new world, it is now therefore no time for men to look to get riches, brave clothes, dainty fare, but to look to present necessities; it is now no time to pamper the flesh, live at ease, snatch, catch, scrape and pill, and hoard up, but rather to open the doors, the chests, the vessels, and say, brother, neighbour, friend, what want ye, anything that I have? Make bold with it, it is yours to command, to do you good, to comfort and cherish you, and glad I am that I have it for you.

Cushman's stirring peroration invoked the migration across the Atlantic as nothing less than a second reformation – not in ecclesiastical matters this time, but in manners, customs and political economy, calling on the settlers to put the Old World behind them, to forget about their status there. 'Look not gapingly one upon another, pleading your goodness, your birth, your life you lived, your means you had and might have had', he pleaded, but instead embrace a new ethos for the New World:

Lay away all thought of former things, and forget them
and think upon the things that are . . . And as you are
a body together, so hang together not by skins and
gymocks, but labour to be joined together and knit by
flesh and sinews; away with envy at the good of others,
and rejoice in his good and sorrow for his evil. Let
his joy be thy joy, and his sorrow thy sorrow: let his
sickness by thy sickness: his hunger thy hunger: his
poverty thy poverty.

He returned to England on the *Fortune*. On the way
home French privateers boarded the ship and hijacked
the cargo, but Cushman preserved his papers, including
the articles of the plantation. Continuing to work for
the colony, he helped to prepare *Mourt's Relation*, a
promotional account of the Separatists' first winter in
Plymouth. Published in 1622, the book included a
powerful essay by Cushman arguing the case for
emigration to Massachusetts. Among the moral imperatives offered as inducements he offered this précis of his
sermon in Plymouth:

A man must not respect only to live, and do good to
himself, but he should see where he can live to do most
good to others; for, as one saith, 'He whose living is but
for himself, it is time he were dead.'

Mourt's Relation was more or less required reading for
the English Puritans during the 1620s. John Winthrop,
pondering his own possible move to Massachusetts,
almost certainly knew it well. He might even have seen a

manuscript version of 'The Sin and Danger of Self Love' itself. So when it fell to him to inspire his own plantation with a stirring sermon, he must have had Cushman's theme firmly fixed in his mind.

As befitted the better-educated speaker and audience, Winthrop's version of the Great American Speech had a more learned air than Cushman's. There were far more references to scripture – well beyond the number required to establish the argument – and Winthrop's diction was more abstract and polysyllabic. Where Cushman got the idea across with a concrete example – 'hath he no bed to lie on? Why, I have two, I'll lend him one' – Winthrop used 'abridge ourselves of our superfluities for the supply of others' necessities'. This is what made Cushman by far the better prose stylist, and almost certainly – we can only guess – the better public speaker.

Yet for all their different levels of style, their themes had much in common. Both took as their model St Paul's figure of the church as the body of Christ. Indeed, for Winthrop this was the governing motif. 'All the parts of this body . . . must needs partake of each other's strength and infirmity, joy and sorrow, weal and woe.'

From the church as the body of Christ it is a short step to the so-called primitive church, Christians in the apostolic era who lived with the minimum of govern-ment. Both speakers adopted this model. Thus Winthrop: 'In the primitive Church they sold all, had all things in common.' And Cushman: 'And Paul sought no man's gold nor silver, but though he had authority, yet he took not bread of the churches, but laboured with his hands.'

The New World called for a new morality. 'Whatsoever we did, or ought to have done, when we lived in England', said Winthrop, the same must we do, and more also . . . We must bear one another's burdens. We must not look only on our own things, but also on the things of our brethren.'

But on the edge of a vast wilderness, the New World also held its terrors. Their exposed position, far from putting them anxiously on guard against one another, should free the colonists' generosity. 'Community of peril calls for extraordinary liberality', Winthrop taught, and so that 'our Christian brother may be relieved of his distress, we must help him beyond our ability'.

Christian love was a universal, timeless value that underpinned the Commonwealth. And private enterprise was not a gratification to be allowed after the straitened early days of the common struggle, but an integral part of mankind's fallen state:

Adam in his first estate was a perfect model of mankind . . . But Adam himself rent from his Creator, rent all his posterity also one from another; whence it comes that every man is born with this principle in him to love and seek himself only; and thus a man continueth till Christ comes and takes possession of the soul and infuseth another principle, love to God and our brother.

So while Cushman outlined the ideals, Winthrop turned them into a statement of national – or certainly communal – cultural identity. No wonder later historians

and other guardians of the nation's identity have overlooked, misunderstood or had to reinvent Winthrop
as the precursor to American independence. Private
enterprise as a direct result of the Fall? The idea just
couldn't be squared with the nation's dominant identity.

Not that it mattered. Even while Robert Cushman was
speaking to the settlers at Plymouth, he was interrupted
by objections that, left to their own consciences, the lazier
settlers would just lie around doing nothing, while their
more responsible comrades did all the work. And at least
one of the Massachusetts Bay settlers was driven to
thoughts of suicide after attempting to live up to the
ideals of commonwealth so encouraged by Cushman and
Winthrop. This was John Dane, a Hertfordshire tailor
who settled in Massachusetts in the 1630s. He brought
with him a year's supply of food. Following Winthrop's
lead (and Cushman's before him), he began to give it away
to those in greater need than he. 'I thought if one had it,
another should not want', he wrote in his autobiography
two years before he died in 1684. 'There came a neighbor
to me and said he had no corn', he recalled. 'He made
great complaints. I told him I had one bushel and I had
no more, but he should have half of it.' Later Dane
discovered that 'at the same time he had a bushel in his
house. It troubled me to see his dealings and the dealings
of other men.'

Like Winthrop, Dane had expected that a New World
would give birth to a new morality. Instead, people
seemed to be carrying on much as before. This dis-
enchantment, together with other 'troubles I passed
through', led him to despair:

I found in my heart that I could not serve God as I should . . . Upon a time, walking with my gun on my shoulder charged, in the mile brook path, beyond Deacon Goodhewe's, I had several thoughts came flocking into my mind, that I had better make away with myself than to live longer . . . I cock[ed] my gun and set it on the ground, and put the muzzle under my throat, and took up my foot to let it off.[2]

Though 'at that time [he] no more scrupled to kill [him]self than to go home to [his] own house', he did not pull the trigger, but instead began to think that God's blessedness 'might belong' to him, 'and it much supported my spirit'.

Just two years after Cushman's sermon, Plymouth Plantation abandoned its communitarianism. As William Bradford, governor of the colony, tells the story in his journal/history *Of Plymouth Plantation* (written between 1630 and 1647), discontent at the idleness of some members of the plantation forced him to agree to allow everyone 'to set corn . . . for his own particular'.

This reversion to private enterprise succeeded handsomely, 'for it made all hands very industrious, so as much more corn was planted than otherwise', and even 'the women now went willingly into the field, and took their little ones with them to set corn'. Thus child labour came to the New World.

PART TWO

The Great American Speech

G reat American Speeches are part of the culture: monumental not just in tone and breadth of reference, but often literally. Some have accompanied the dedication of monuments, like Daniel Webster's at Bunker Hill or Lincoln's at Gettysburg. Others have themselves become monuments, their words carved in stone, as behind the great statue of the seated president inside the Lincoln Memorial in Washington, or 'Ask not what your country can do for you' carved in granite at John F. Kennedy's gravesite in Arlington Cemetery, just across the Potomac.

To be remembered, not to say monumentalized, the speech has to have several qualities. To start with, it has to be a real speech, a live performance heard and shared by both audience and speaker. The hearers need to pick up the speaker's tone as well as his or her content, and to share the experience with others in the audience. Speakers need feedback from their audience, in the form of applause, or signs of boredom, irritation or even hostility. So these criteria exclude even those celebrated talks like Franklin D. Roosevelt's Fireside Chats over the radio, or John F. Kennedy's crucial radio and television address delivered from the Oval Office on 11 June 1963, in which he proposed the Civil Rights Act of 1964.

As for what it's about and how it's put together, the Great American Speech tends to conform to a pattern in subject-matter, tone and mode of argument. First of all, it has to be about America. It has to offer hope for the future. Above all, it should say something about how Americans could be good, or better: by transcending differences of race, class, success, wealth and fortune generally. More often than not, the proffered route to reformation is reversion to America's founding principles, especially the golden sentence in the Declaration of Independence that 'all men are created equal.'

It follows from this formulation that the Great American Speech is not partisan, does not reference the quotidian, however it might be motivated by pressing current pressures. Therefore campaign addresses do not qualify; nor do congressional speeches for or against a particular piece of legislation. So if not campaigns or the day-to-day dialectic of public policy, what sort of events have prompted the Great American Speech? These tend to be occasions calling for praise, reflection, retrospection or projection, like inaugural addresses of presidents about to enter office, Fourth of July orations celebrating the country's anniversary, speeches in memory of the dead – say, at the dedication of a memorial – and those most American of oratorical forms and occasions, the commencement address delivered to the graduands of a university.

Can it be ghostwritten? This is a vexed issue. Of the great monumental speech-makers considered here, John

Adams, Thomas Jefferson, Daniel Webster and Abraham Lincoln largely wrote their own speeches. Of these, Lincoln was the most humane, imaginative and philosophically astute. He was also the most gifted and practised rhetorician. Since then, writes Fred Kaplan in his fine study of Lincoln's literary style, 'The articulation of a modern president's vision and policies has fallen to speech-writers and speech-writing committees, with the president serving, at best, as editor in chief.'

Some of these ghostwriters, such as those working for Franklin D. Roosevelt and John F. Kennedy, have been better than others, Kaplan concedes, but 'the challenge of a president himself struggling to find the conjunction between the right words and honest expression, a use of language that respects intellect, truth, and sincerity, has been largely abandoned'[1]

It is true that Lincoln's linguistic powers could hardly have found their full expression if his speeches had been written by a committee. But it doesn't work the other way round – not as a general rule anyway. Solo authorship does not guarantee quality; any faults in the speaker's character, intellect, logic or rhetoric will stand out all the more glaringly if not edited or otherwise tempered by an assistant. Besides, there is at least one known case in which Lincoln acted more as editor than originator, his First Inaugural Address, part of which was first drafted by his secretary of state, William Seward. Lincoln's emendations were a vast improvement on Seward's draft, yet the element of collaboration was still there.

It is probably wrong, too, to infer a pattern of decline over time in the history of American presidential oratory.

For one thing, speech-writers came on board surprisingly early, starting with Alexander Hamilton, who wrote much of George Washington's celebrated Farewell Address of 1796. And by the 1830s the project had already become a team effort by the president and his close associates. Andrew Jackson, president from 1829 to 1837, drew on the help of advisors like Francis Blair, Amos Kendall, Andrew Donelson and Roger Taney to compose his speeches and other pronouncements. His political opponents called these men Jackson's 'kitchen cabinet', implying that that they entered the White House for informal discussions by the back door leading to the kitchen, rather than the more ceremonial entrance to the parlour.

Together they produced statements like Jackson's message to the Senate of 10 July 1832, vetoing Congress's re-authorization of the Second National Bank of the u.s. – not a speech, to be sure (though widely circulated in the press), but a monument of another kind, since it altered the course of American constitutional history, adding greatly to the power of the Executive as the direct representative of the People. According to the senior historian of Jackson and his presidency, it was 'the most important presidential veto in American history' and 'a powerful and dramatic polemic, cleverly written to appeal to the great masses of the people and to convince them of its arguments'.[2] Yet it was a collaboration. The ideas and arguments started with Jackson himself; much of the first draft was by Amos Kendall, with Donelson, Taney and secretary of the Navy Levi Woodbury assisting.

'Except for Washington's farewell address and Jefferson's pre-presidential Declaration of Independence', writes Kaplan, 'few presidents' words before Lincoln and very few after have presence, let alone residue, in the American national memory.' Yet Washington's farewell address too was a collaboration. 'Some of Franklin Roosevelt's words have struck deeply into the American consciousness, not because he wrote them but because at a time of national crisis he assembled the best team of speech-writers of any modern president and worked closely with them.'[3]

Exactly. In other words, whether or not a presidential statement becomes a monument has little bearing on its literal, line by line authorship. There must be some congruence between the speech and the president's character, interests and policy, of course, but then good advisors soon pick up what their man wants and how he thinks.

This point can best be illustrated, oddly enough, by a fragment from a British speech, which has become something of a monument in its own right. On 10 October 1980 at their annual party conference, British premier and leader of the Conservative Party Margaret Thatcher famously rebuffed the suggestion that she should rein in the free-market reforms that had put the economy in recession and helped to increase unemployment to over two million. 'To those waiting with bated breath', she said, 'for that favourite media catchphrase "U-turn", I have only one thing to say: You turn if you want to. The lady's not for turning.'

The remark, written by her speechwriter, Sir Ronald Millar, punned on the title of a verse comedy of 1949 by Christopher Fry, *The Lady's Not for Burning*. Thatcher had never heard of either play or playwright, and she didn't get the joke even after it was explained to her. But so closely did the reference encapsulate her spirit and policies that it produced a rapturous standing ovation lasting over five minutes, and has remained in the public memory as a byword for her character in office.

As in Great Britain, so in the United States. There is no marked correlation between single authorship and the question of whether the finished product lives on in the public consciousness. Like great movies, Great American Speeches exist in themselves, as events. But unlike the British, Americans carve these great words in stone. Those monuments in Washington, DC, which enshrine the Great American Speeches they most want to remember, can serve as reminders of their better nature, their true founding principles.

3

Inaugurals: Adams, Jefferson and America's First Parties

THROUGHOUT THE EIGHTEENTH and most of the nineteenth centuries presidents did not speak to Congress in the ordinary business of American government from day to day, or even year to year. They communicated through written executive orders and proclamations. So there were no State of the Union addresses. 'Special Messages', as they were called then, were written, not spoken.

As for speaking directly to the people, that was thought to be little better than demagoguery. Franklin D. Roosevelt's 'Fireside Chats' and John F. Kennedy's televised policy proposals would have been unthinkable – and not just because the technology was lacking. When Andrew Jackson tried to go over the head of Congress to appeal directly to the people to reinforce his hostility to the Second National Bank of the U.S., Senator Daniel Webster reacted vehemently:

But if the President were now to meet us with a speech, and should inform us of measures . . . which should appear to use the most plain, palpable, and dangerous violation of the Constitution, we must,

nevertheless, either keep respectful silence, or fill our
answer merely with courtly phrases of approbation.[1]

What Webster feared was that in speaking direct, whether
to Congress or to the people, Jackson would exceed his
powers in the delicate balance between Executive,
Legislature and Judiciary, all three of which were furiously
engaged in the so-called Bank War of 1831–4. This idea
of the separation of powers goes back to antiquity, but is a
famous principle of the u.s. Constitution as framed, and
as defended by the Federalist Papers, a series of 85 articles
and essays written by Alexander Hamilton, James
Madison and John Jay, published in the *Independent
Journal* and the *New York Packet* between October 1787
and August 1788.

In Federalist Paper 49 Madison warns against 'the
danger of disturbing the public tranquillity by interesting
too strongly the public passions'. Normally these would
most likely be stirred up by the legislature, since 'their
connections of blood, of friendship and of acquaintance,
embrace a great proportion of the most influential part
of the society'. But 'the executive power might be in the
hands of a peculiar favorite of the people', in which case
'the public decision might be less swayed by prepossus-
sions in favor of the legislative party'. Either way, he
added, public feeling thus aroused 'could never be
expected to turn on the true merits of the question'.[2]

Presidential speeches to the populace at large had
to wait until the twentieth century. In *The Rhetorical
Presidency* (1987) Jeffrey Tulis argues that it was Theodore
Roosevelt, president from 1901 to 1909, and Woodrow

Wilson, 1913–21, who made the transition from the traditional role of the presidency to the twentieth-century style of addressing the people directly. Roosevelt began to speak directly to the people, urging 'moderate appeals for moderate reform'. With Woodrow Wilson, Tulis explains, 'truly important speeches would be delivered orally, where the visible and audible performance would become as important as the prepared text'. Wilson developed two kinds of presidential speech still common today, the 'visionary' address that would 'articulate a picture of the future and impel a populace towards it', and the 'policy-stand' speech, which communicates 'where the president stood or what he would do regarding issues of the day'.[3]

Of the Great American Speeches examined here, only those by John Fitzgerald Kennedy come close to fitting these categories. His Inaugural Address of 1961, hinting at rapprochement with the USSR and even a distant end to the Cold War, can certainly be called visionary. His commencement address to the graduands of American University on 10 June 1963 is also visionary in its continued prospect of better Soviet–American relations, but it announced two aspects of policy: his intention to go to Moscow to meet Premier Khrushchev and British Prime Minister Harold Macmillan and an immediate American unilateral suspension of nuclear tests in the atmosphere.

Of the other speeches here, that of Martin Luther King Jr was certainly visionary, as its often repeated and best remembered phrase, 'I have a dream' clearly pro-claimed, but it also proposed tactics for the near future of the civil rights campaign, and warned against allowing 'our creative protest to degenerate into physical violence'. As for Daniel Webster's dedication of the Bunker Hill Memorial and Abraham Lincoln's Gettysburg Address, they both offered visions of a better future, but grounded their hope and persuasion on a reflection of America's past.

In any case, the one exception to the early prohibition of presidents speaking straight to the people was the inaugural address. This wasn't yet the great speech delivered from the Capitol Building by such as Franklin Delano Roosevelt, John F. Kennedy and Barack Obama to crowds massed below. It often took place indoors, to an invited audience. Still, it was the Great American Speech as we have defined it.

You might think that few political debates would have divided the American Republic in its early days. Following the Revolutionary War – or War of Independence, to give the violent schism from Great Britain its more conservative name – people were too busy, surely, building a new political order and exploring the delights of their newfound continent to squabble amongst themselves. You would be wrong. The very novelty of the national enterprise made its citizens nervous. A false step in framing the Constitution, or in calculating the relative power of the individual states as against the Federal Government, or in a dozen other founding judgements could bring the whole edifice down, leaving it vulnerable to the hostile European monarchies just itching for the new country to fail.

Besides, this was some time before Anglo-Saxon politics had settled into the pattern of government and opposition, two or more parties of roughly equal power that agree on the fundamental structures of the country's management while disputing specific policies. The concept of a *loyal* opposition had yet to emerge. In eighteenth-century England the opposition was a faction (as Dr Johnson's dictionary defined the Whigs); in America it might be a bomb planted in the country's foundations.

This fear of faction had been the theme of George Washington's farewell message of 1796. As 'the father of his country' – the colonials' commanding officer during the Revolutionary War and the new country's first president – Washington's prestige was immense. Above all, he warned of the future danger of sectionalism within the federal union. 'The name of American, which belongs to you in your national capacity', he said, 'must always exalt the just pride of patriotism more than any appellation derived from local discriminations. With slight shades of difference, you have the same religion, manners, habits and political principles.'

Sectionalism could take many forms. It could emerge as friction between the states, and between whole regions: north versus south; east against west. Or it could develop as contradictions between the kind of local government exercised by the individual states and the federal power wielded centrally, first in Philadelphia, then soon in Washington, DC, a tension leading at worst to one or more states wanting to secede from the Union. Or various sections of the country might choose different sides in a foreign war, like the one currently raging between France and Great Britain. As it happened, all these threats would materialize in time, the last almost immediately.

And what might be the vehicle for these sectionalist tendencies? Their most likely source, the most immediate cause of division, would be established political parties. 'The spirit of party' itself, Washington warned, has 'its root in the strongest passions of the human mind'. And when one party takes the place of another following a democratic vote, party loyalties are 'sharpened by the spirit of revenge' until 'the minds of men ... seek security and repose in the absolute power of an individual; and sooner or later the chief of some prevailing faction, more able or more fortunate than his competitors, turns this disposition to the purposes of his own elevation, on the ruins of public liberty.'

Washington's fears for a sectional future were plausible enough in a country already grown so big and so diverse in its social and physical environments. But it was already too late to prevent the emergence of political parties. By the time Washington's vice president John Adams succeeded him as president in his own right, the voters were torn between two parties more radically distinct in their policies, their class affiliation and even their regional base than at any time since in American politics. And it was all the work of the so-called Founding Fathers, those great geniuses of legal and institutional framing.

What happened was this. During his tenure as Washington's Secretary of the Treasury Alexander Hamilton had worked out a strategy to make the United States an economic power capable of dealing four-square with the established powers of Europe. To make the United States creditworthy, so that investors felt secure in buying its bonds, he introduced a tax on whisky, in order to pay off, at full face value, the national debt run up during the Revolutionary War. He then proposed a new national debt, created a Bank of the United States along the lines of the Bank of England, and imposed a tariff on foreign imports to support domestic manufactures. Finally, he proposed to establish a standing army. Accordingly, in as early as 1792 he formed the Federalist Party to promote these policies.

All this beefing up of the federal government was anathema to James Madison, one of the chief theorists of the Constitution, and especially to Thomas Jefferson, who had written most of the Declaration of Independence. They preferred local control to strong centralized government. Jefferson, taking his cue from the French Physiocrats, thought that the securest source of wealth was the natural increase derived from cultivating the land; that the true bedrock of democracy was not banking, business and industrialization, but independent yeomen tilling and improving the farms they owned. So alongside the Federalists they formed an anti-administration group – at first a faction – they called the Republican Party (not to be confused with the present-day American Republican Party, with which it had no connection).

These were profound differences, not just about how to run the country, but in its national identity. Indeed the parties even differed over democracy itself. The Federalists were highly sceptical of what the Constitution calls (as we still do today) 'the people'. They retained that eighteenth-century view of society as hierarchical, with public office reserved, as Hamilton put it frankly, for 'the rich, the able and the well-born'. In fact, as the distinguished American historian Eric Foner has put it, 'The Federalists may have been the only party in American history forthrightly to proclaim democracy and freedom dangerous in the hands of ordinary citizens.'[4]

Republicans were more open to the idea of popular democracy. They were strong on equality, distrusting the 'monarchical' and elitist tendencies of the Federalists' policies. Jefferson believed in the sound common sense of average citizens, especially if they owned land.

Foreign relations also bedevilled the picture. The Federalists, consciously building on a British pattern, favoured close ties with that country, while the Republicans, though far from wanting to model their country on post-revolutionary France, were strongly attracted to its ideals of liberty and equality. The fact that France and Great Britain were at war throughout the period in which American parties were forming made early American party rivalry all the more toxic.

By the time of the presidential election of 1796, the first to be contested, the two parties were well organized and sharply focused on either side of the fierce struggle. At least the candidates for president and vice president represented a reasonable spread of experience and region. The Federalists chose Washington's vice president, John Adams, as their presidential candidate. A lawyer from Massachusetts, he had long been a leading advocate for American independence, and had helped write the Declaration. For the office of vice president they put up Thomas Pinckney, Revolutionary War veteran and former governor of South Carolina.

Running for president on the Republican side was the party's co-founder, the Virginia planter Thomas Jefferson, the chief author of the Declaration, an ardent campaigner for popular democracy and a learned diplomat who could speak five languages fluently. For vice president the Republicans nominated the New York lawyer Aaron Burr, another veteran of the Revolutionary War and grandson of the great Connecticut Valley theological philosopher and revivalist preacher, Jonathan Edwards.

In the event the contest was a bitter one, overshadowed by the parties' supposed sympathies with the warring European nations. Each party accused the other of wanting to undermine the foundations of the new republic. The Federalists, trying to implicate the Republicans in the violence of the French Revolution, called them Jacobins and anarchists, while the Republicans characterized the Federalists as monarchists and even traitors for trying to draw America back into the aristocratic and elitist structures of the old British adversary.

To complicate matters further, Hamilton, always the restless stirrer, began to distrust the true federalism of Adams, who was known to be stubbornly – some said, self-importantly – independent in his political judgements. Although then as now each state was allocated a number of electoral votes proportionate to its number of congressmen, the difference then was that the electors were real people who, following a period of negotiation, coercion or even bribery, might or might not reflect their state's popular vote.

Hamilton realized that though electors from the southern states would almost certainly be voting for

Jefferson, they might be coerced at least into casting their second vote for the South Carolinian Pinckney – to the extent that Pinckney, not Adams, would emerge as head of the Federalist ticket, and thus become president.

Of course, it didn't work out like that, but Hamilton's ploy was sufficient to upset his expectations in a way most retrograde to his desire, to paraphrase Claudius in *Hamlet*. Sure enough, as he wished, all eight of South Carolina's electors cast their ballots for Jefferson and Pinckney, but what he didn't anticipate (and couldn't control) was how many Adams electors would fail to cast their second vote for Pinckney. In those days the candidate receiving the second highest number of votes became vice president. In the event the electoral votes stacked up as follows: Adams, 71 (mainly from the north and east); Jefferson, 68 (mainly from the south, though including Pennsylvania); Pinckney, 59; Burr, 30. Adams, a Federalist (at least nominally), had as his vice president the leading Republican. A curious result, given that the two parties were so radically opposed.

Adams's inauguration took place just before noon on Saturday, 4 March 1797, in the House of Representatives chamber of the gracious Congress Hall, Philadelphia, then the seat of the American legislature. Also present on the raised dais in front of the room were Jefferson, who had already been sworn in as vice president upstairs in the Senate chamber earlier that morning; Oliver Ellsworth, the chief justice of the Supreme Court, who would administer the oath of office; and the outgoing president, General George Washington himself.

The hall was packed to the rafters with members (and their wives) of the House and Senate, the government bureaucracy, the diplomatic corps and others. Adams delivered his address before being sworn in. He is said to have spoken in a loud, clear voice and to have moved the audience repeatedly to tears, though this may have had less to do with the speech than with the momentous occasion on which it was delivered. After all, here were three of the chief architects of the new country gathered before the rest of the government, and what with Washington's retirement, perhaps together for the last time.

What sort of speech should an inaugural address be? The only precedents were George Washington's two, one for each term he served. His first expressed his sense of inadequacy in the face of the task, invoking the support of his fellow citizens and the Almighty, and refusing to take any pay for the job beyond expenses. His second, weighing in at 135 words, still holds the record for the shortest ever given.

But since Washington had been elected unopposed, these self-effacing gestures couldn't be taken as models. What kind of inaugural address might follow a bitter struggle between two parties sharing so little common ground? Should it be a strenuous prospectus of policies to be enacted by the winning party? Should it be tauntingly triumphalist in tone, exhibiting that 'spirit of revenge' so deprecated by Washington in his farewell message?

Not to worry. Adams could hardly have thought such a message or tone appropriate, not with Washington sitting beside him. Besides, it is a basic rule of democracies that though elected by only part of the citizenry, the successful candidate has to serve all of it. Even Margaret Thatcher, that most divisive of British prime ministers, entered

Downing Street paraphrasing a prayer supposedly composed (though actually not) by St Francis of Assisi: 'Where there is discord, may we bring harmony.'[5]

In any case and for whatever reason, Adams's speech was the opposite of partisan – but strenuously so, as if he were struggling to rein himself in. He avoided factionalism by talking about the things on which they could all agree: the superiority of the new Constitution over the old Articles of Confederation, the justice and vigour of American democracy, and the prudence, temperance and fortitude of the outgoing president, General Washington. Indeed, apart from the lengthy list of pledges for his future service to the country, the speech belonged almost completely to what rhetoricians (following Aristotle's *Rhetoric*) call the epideictic branch of oratory – that is, occupied with praise of the present.

It must have been hard to follow when heard, so tightly wrought is it, its syntax woven so intricately. It's certainly highly rhetorical. So, for example, he describes the purpose of the new Constitution as 'to form a more perfect union, establish justice, insure domestic tranquility, provide for the common defense, promote the general welfare, and secure the blessings of liberty'. Since several of these accomplishments – numbers three, five and six in the series – amount to much the same thing, we must take it that the series has been multiplied to fatten out the isocolon, or repetition of clauses of the same grammatical structure and roughly the same length.

Adams was something of an expert on constitutions, having largely written that of his native state, Massachusetts, and produced a book on the subject.[6] In 1787, when the Philadelphia Convention was framing the American Constitution, he was living in London, serving as America's first ambassador to the Court of St James. Did he feel cut off from this crucial moment in the development of his country's government? Possibly, though his book had made its contribution, having been read and admired by Jefferson, then living in Paris as American minister to France, and by Dr Benjamin Rush, another Founding Father, who led Pennsylvania's ratification of the Constitution. And certainly the Constitution as it emerged, with its bicameral congress and clear separation of powers between executive and legislature, fitted Adams's own beliefs.

So on the surface, at least, his account of first reading the new constitution is equable in tone:

> Employed in the service of my country abroad during the whole course of these transactions [to frame the document], I first saw the Constitution of the United States in a foreign country. Irritated by no literary altercation, animated by no public debate, heated by no party animosity, I read it with great satisfaction, as the result of good heads prompted by good hearts, as an experiment better adapted to the genius, character, situation, and relations of this nation and country than any which had ever been proposed or suggested.

On show here are two of Adams's most characteristic stylistic traits: first, as in the preceding paragraph, the insistent isocolon, and second his fondness for participial constructions ('employed'; 'irritated'; 'animated'; 'heated').

Of course, the participles all point to the same subject, John Adams, and the repetition of clauses makes his reaction sound momentous. But offsetting that emphasis is the fact that what is being repeated is a series of negatives – preconceptions and emotions he didn't bring to the experience. And the same goes for two further formulations later in the paragraph:

> It was not then, nor has been since, any objection to it in my mind that the Executive and Senate were not more permanent. Nor have I ever entertained a thought of promoting any alteration in it but such as the people themselves . . . should see and feel to be necessary . . .

Of course, the absence of partisanship underscores his admirable neutrality, but it is almost as though these phrases hint at what he *might* have felt and thought, or more likely what his compatriots might have *suspected* him of feeling and thinking, over there, across the Atlantic, so out of the American current. Certainly Adams favoured a strong executive – his enemies even accused him of wanting a hereditary president, and to be grooming his son, John Quincy, as his heir – and when he first saw the Constitution, he wrote to Jefferson in Paris that it ought to have included a bill of rights.

In any case, there is nothing of this self-enforced neutrality in his sense that the document suits the nation, or in his happy compressed anaphora, 'good heads prompted by good hearts'. And when later in the speech he comes to a comparison between American democracy and the inherited privilege of the Old World, his rhetoric of praise rises to an artful crescendo:

> Can anything essential, anything more than mere ornament and decoration, be added to this by robes and diamonds? Can authority be more amiable and respectable when it descends from accidents or institutions established in remote antiquity than when it springs fresh from the hearts and judgments of an honest and enlightened people?

This is masterful. Set against the 'springs' and 'fresh' and 'hearts' of the American polity, 'descends' is made to sound more like stale decline than orderly succession. 'Accidents' is especially well chosen because it reminds his audience of the often haphazard foundation on which the cumbersome edifice of the divine right of inherited monarchy rests. As Thomas Paine put it in his *Common Sense* (1776), 'A French bastard landing with an armed banditti, and establishing himself king of England against the consent of the natives, is in plain terms a very paltry rascally original. It certainly hath no divinity in it.' But 'accidents' can also be taken in its philosophical sense, as opposed to substance: that is, the properties of a thing not essential to its nature, like the baubles of 'robes and diamonds'.

In other words, though we know Adams had some doubts about the Constitution as it emerged, when it came to his inaugural, his criticism had to hang fire, even if his praise had to be hissed through the clenched teeth of his denied partisanship. But when it came to his native land, his praise was unreserved, fluid and eloquently stated; the prose runs free in a series of rhetorical questions.

And the youth of his country provided a happy leitmotif when he came to his eulogy of George Washington, in the twilight of whose retirement he is careful to weave the dawn of America's promise: 'May he long live to enjoy the delicious recollections of his services, the gratitude of mankind, the happy fruits of them to himself and the world, which are daily increasing, and that splendid prospect of the future fortunes of this country, which are opening from year to year.'

Adams left for last the only real business of an inaugural address – at least as the genre developed over time – his commitment to the task ahead. He preserves just the ghost of Washington's self-depreciation, in that all the talents and attainments he claims to bring to the job are expressed conditionally – literally in the form of a long string of clauses beginning with 'If . . .'. This one is typical: 'If an inclination to improve agriculture, commerce and manufactures for necessity, convenience and defense . . .'. Less expected, because Adams was nominally a Federalist, was 'If a personal esteem for the French nation . . .', but then this impartiality was becoming the tone of inaugural addresses.

There are seventeen such subordinate clauses in all, leading finally to the main clause: 'It shall be my strenuous endeavour that this sagacious injunction of the two houses shall not be without effect.' In other words, *if* he really possesses all those talents, convictions and good intentions for his presidential career, he will put to good use the electors' invitation to take up the post. But coming at the end of a 689-word sentence, this rhetorically weak, wordy pay-off hardly works as a peroration. Whereas you would expect to find the most important information in the main clause, it is all in the subordinate constructions instead. Yet with each hedged about with conditionality, the effect is strategic humility worthy of Uriah Heep. Overall it is a highly egocentric discourse, one whose syntax – those repeated participles, that long series of conditional clauses – points to and builds up suspense for the disclosure of me, me, me. Yet it does the work of the Great American Speech, the celebration of what brings Americans together, if only through suppressing any hint of partisanship.

As president, Adams retained most of Washington's cabinet and policies, while frequently taking an independent line from that of his advisors. During his only term a diplomatic crisis blew up with France, threatening a war that Hamilton and other Federalists did their best to inflame, but Adams averted. A more serious controversy blew up over the Alien and Sedition Acts of 1798, a nakedly partisan move against the Republican Party.

The Alien Act made it possible for federal authorities to deport 'dangerous aliens', because many recent immigrants – some French, or sympathetic to the French Revolution – naturally gravitated to the Republican Party. The Sedition Act facilitated the suppression of virtually any pamphlet, periodical or public meeting critical of the government. The Republicans were outraged at what they argued was a violation of the First Amendment of the Constitution, prohibiting Congress from making any law 'abridging the freedom of speech, or of the press; or the right of the people peaceably to assemble'. Jefferson compared the new laws to the Salem witch trials.

The election campaign of 1800 was one of the bitterest in American history. The parties were more entrenched now, with the pro-British Federalists favouring strong central government and the pro-French Republicans favouring decentralization. As before, each party accused the other of wanting to bring ruin upon the other, if not upon the whole country. Once again Adams ran as the Federalist candidate alongside Pinckney, and once again Hamilton schemed against the former to get the latter elected. Once again Jefferson and Burr headed up the Republican ticket, only this time the Republicans won, with both the victorious president and vice president coming from the same party.

Resentment at taxes levied to build up the federal army and suspicion in the wake of the Alien and Sedition Acts swung the electorate towards the Republicans. In addition the Federalists were split and the Republicans better organized. In Electoral College votes the result was close, with Jefferson winning 73 as against Adams's 65, but the Republican's share of the popular vote was much greater, at 61.4 per cent against the Federalist's 38.8.

Thomas Jefferson was sworn in on 4 March 1801 for what would be the first of his two terms. By this time the government had moved from Philadelphia to Washington, so the ceremony took place in the Senate Chamber of the uncompleted Capitol Building. The president elect, dressed as an ordinary citizen, with no badge of rank or ceremonial sword, walked from his boarding house up Capitol Hill. Well over a thousand men and women crowded into the hall. John Adams was not among them. He had left Washington for his home in Quincy, Massachusetts, early on the same day, bitterly disappointed at the outcome of the election and crushed by the recent death of his son Charles.

Jefferson's speech was delivered 'in so low a tone that few heard it', according to one observer. In any case, he had taken the precaution to give a copy to the editor of the *National Intelligencer* so that a printed version could be handed out to the audience on their way out of the Senate Chamber. It was later distributed widely in pamphlet and broadside form, as well as in newspapers across the country and in the London *Times* and *Monthly Magazine.*

After such a fierce contest, you might expect Jefferson's first inaugural to break from the neutrality that was already becoming the norm. Far from it. Although identifiably Republican in promising limited central government and praising the state governments 'as the most competent administrations for our domestic concerns', it rang out a clear plea for reconciliation between the warring parties.

The election has been characterized by its 'animation of discussions and of exertions', he admits, in what must have seemed the understatement of the decade. 'Strangers unused to think freely and to write what they think', he says, might even have been taken aback by it. But now that the issue has been decided 'by the voice of the nation, . . . all will, of course . . . unite in common efforts for the common good'.

Jefferson did not utter that word 'common' lightly. His first draft had 'public good' for 'common good', but he changed that to repeat the word for emphasis. Because, as he goes on to show, the warring parties, for all their differences, really do share a common ground:

> But every difference of opinion is not a difference of principle. We have called by different names brethren of the same principle. We are all Republicans, we are all Federalists.

This is the most famous part of the speech, and he went to some pains to produce it. His first draft had:

> But let it not be imagined that every difference of opinion or of feelings is a difference of principle, we have called by different names modificns [*sic*] of the same principle. we are all republicans: we are all federalists.

So the final version has been pruned to focus the central proposition, and to bring the seeming antithesis of 'republicans' and 'federalists' into sharper relief. But equally important is that the rather dully taxonomic 'modific[atio]ns' has been replaced by the familial 'brethren', a striking endorsement of his thesis.

But what did he mean? Was this equivalence of parties anything more than a warm bath of words to suit the bipartisan occasion? Yes it was, and his rationale of the apparent paradox is more explicit in the first draft. We are 'all Federalists' for the simple reason that no 'native citizen

in the U.S. . . . wishes to dissolve this union.' We are
Republicans because 'there are few native citizens who
wish to change it's [*sic*] republican features' – that is,
revert to a monarchy.

In the final version Jefferson expands his opinion that
no one would want to break up the Union. This addition
is perhaps the most important passage in the speech:

> If there be any among us who would wish to dissolve
> this Union or to change its republican form, let them
> stand as monuments of the safety with which error of
> opinion may be tolerated where reason is left free to
> combat it.

On one level this might be taken as an elegant apodioxis
– the rhetorical ploy of 'I won't dignify that comment
with a serious answer'. Thomas Paine had used the tactic
to great effect in *Common Sense* (1776):

> However, it is needless to spend much time in exposing
> the folly of hereditary right; if there are any so weak
> as to believe it, let them promiscuously worship the
> ass and lion, and welcome. I shall neither copy their
> humility, nor disturb their devotion.

Yet Jefferson's plea could be taken seriously too. In effect,
he is saying something like this: differing as we do in our
opinions, we Federalists and Republicans agree on the
principle that the country should be a federal union
governed by elected representatives, with an elected
president, not a king, at its head. But if there are any who

do not accept even this principle, then we must take there to be an even deeper foundation to our polity – our basic tolerance and fellowship within a rational community.

This concept of principles underlying and shared by two competing parties comes close to inventing our more modern idea of government and opposition, as opposed to the earlier model of government and faction. But Jefferson goes even further than this. What he is proposing is that even those who reject the principles underlying national identity could be tolerated within the American sphere. Or to put it another way, the American way can be widened to accommodate even those formally opposed to it.

In this opinion he is following an important essay by his friend and co-founder of the Republican party, James Madison. In the tenth of the *Federalist Papers* Madison had argued that any number of citizens, whether a minority or a majority, representing 'some common impulse of passion, or of interest, adverse to the rights of other citizens, or to the permanent and aggregate interests of the community', would have to be neutralized if the Republic were to run smoothly.

How? Well, you could try 'destroying the liberty which is essential to [the group's] existence', Madison wrote, but since that same liberty 'is essential to political life', that would be to apply a remedy 'worse than the disease'. The wiser course would be to 'control [the] effects' of the pressure group by 'extend[ing] the sphere' of the polity: first, by distancing electors from the levers of power through the ground rules of a republic, where citizens are represented by elected delegates to the executive and legislature; and second, because 'the greater number of citizens and extent of territory which may be brought within the compass' of the Republic as the country expands will dilute the group's impact with interests of their own.[7]

This may explain why at this point, following the discussion of opinions, principles and toleration of the unaccommodated, Jefferson's Inaugural Address moves on to a visionary prospect of the land that all these parties inhabit:

> Let us, then, with courage and confidence pursue our own Federal and Republican principles, our attachment to union and representative government. Kindly separated by nature and a wide ocean from the exterminating havoc of one quarter of the globe, too high-minded to endure the degradation of the others; possessing a chosen country with room enough for our descendants to the thousandth and thousandth generation;

Praise of the country was conventional enough; it was one of those uncontroversial topics guaranteed to elicit unanimous support. Adams before him had included a peon to the nation in his Inaugural Address. But this comes further on in Jefferson's speech than does the equivalent in Adams's, and it is about country – including its geography – as much as it is about nation. Or to put it more exactly, it is about the political constitution as grounded upon its physical nature. Separated by the Atlantic Ocean, the country can avoid the murderous conflicts of Europe. The vast continent before them will provide room for an endless stream of future inhabitants. As the sphere extends, to paraphrase Madison, so an unstressed population will find the confidence to tolerate difference.

4

Webster and Lincoln: Monuments and Memory

A COMMON THEME from the earliest to at least mid-nineteenth-century American speeches is the American project itself. For Daniel Webster, speaking at the end of the so-called 'era of good feelings', the United States were a beacon to the world, whereas Abraham Lincoln in the midst of the Civil War wondered whether a democratic republic could survive.

These two speeches form a great contrast, not least in their bulk. Daniel Webster's 'oration' at the dedication of the Bunker Hill Monument on 17 June 1825, is over 7,600 words long and took two hours to deliver – a monumental speech to celebrate a monument. Abraham Lincoln's Gettysburg Address is a mere 266 words and was over in about three minutes. Yet each in its way is highly conventional, even formal.

Daniel Webster's more obviously. The occasion was the ceremony to mark the fiftieth anniversary of the Battle of Bunker Hill, for Bostonians the pivotal engagement in the Revolutionary War. With the British occupying Boston, colonial forces had moved onto Bunker Hill and Breed's Hill above Charlestown, across the Charles River from what is now downtown Boston, intending to bombard the city and drive the British out. Instead, the British forces mounted three infantry assaults, finally taking both hills by 5 p.m. on the afternoon of 17 June 1775. But thanks to the sharp shooting of the colonials the British victory was a pyrrhic one, leaving them with over 1,000 casualties, including a disproportionate number of officers, compared to 450 on the local side.

Now the city was gathered to lay the cornerstone of what would grow to become a granite obelisk over 220 ft high to mark the site of the battle. The dedication was bound to be a momentous event. Over 20,000 people gathered at the foot of Breed's Hill, among them veterans of the battle itself, now in their seventies and eighties. Also present was the Marquis de Lafayette, an early supporter of American independence, who had served as a major general in the Continental Army under Washington, and whom President James Monroe had invited back as the 'guest of the nation' for an honorary tour. After a funeral march to commemorate the dead, followed by anthems and prayers, Webster rose to speak.

He had been an obvious choice to give the chief oration. A keen lawyer who had argued several key cases before the Supreme Court, Webster had also served in the House of Representatives and the Senate, and would go on to be secretary of state under three presidents.

From the outset Webster struck a tone of religious observance, generated by biblical and liturgical language. 'We are among the sepulchers of our fathers', he said of the ground on which they stood. 'Behold, how altered' is the present scene from the battlefield of fifty years earlier. As for that battle, how should it be remembered? 'Let it not be supposed that our object is to perpetuate national hostility, or even to cherish a mere military spirit. It is higher, purer, nobler. We consecrate our work to the spirit of national independence, and we wish that the light of peace may rest upon it forever.' Later, as if to validate his prescription, he referred to 'this consecrated spot'.

This is what the historian Craig R. Smith calls 'the oratory of civil religion'. After the War of 1812 had consolidated the gains of the Revolution, putting an end to armed conflict with Britain, there arose a second generation of 'orator leaders [who] had a deep belief in the heroic nature of the birth of the United States' – men like Webster, John C. Calhoun and Henry Clay. 'By civil religion', writes Smith, 'I mean the mythos and rhetoric of nation-building that constitute a schema of values which in turn guides decision making.' The national objects of such veneration could displace those of more conventional religion. 'The Union was Webster's heaven on earth', writes Smith, and 'the Constitution was his Ten Commandments.'[1]

Webster's devout respect for the Union would play out in day-to-day politics as part of his intense federalism: his belief in strong central government, his pro-business policies, his advocacy of a national bank, against the determination of Andrew Jackson and the western Democrats to destroy it. But here, in this largely celebratory discourse, his evocation of the Union is much less partisan than that, standing for the country as a whole.

His worshipful mood about the democratic founda-tions and continuing polity of America, together with a widespread optimism about the country's rapid progress, lead here to an intriguing relationship between past, present and future. 'When has it happened that history has had so much to record in the same term of years, as since the seventeenth of June, 1775?' In just fifty years our revolution has been completed, 24 states and a federal government established, and the population grown from two or three to twelve million, now spreading to 'the banks of the Ohio and the Mississippi'.

So quickly has all this been achieved that the past is still with us. Even as we 'look abroad on the brightened prospects of the world . . . we hold still among us some of those who were active agents in the scenes of 1775'. These are the veterans, whom he apostrophizes as 'Venerable men!' They 'have come down to us from a former generation' whose lives 'heaven has bounteously lengthened' so that they 'might behold this joyous day'. Lafayette is even more remarkable, connecting as he does not only 'two generations' but 'both hemispheres'. Time and space seem almost to have collapsed.

Yet, held briefly in the same frame, the two generations prompted a distinction in their function: fighters and framers as against defenders and developers. We of the generation of 1825 can no longer gain renown in a war for independence, nor can we sit 'at the side of Solon and Alfred, and other founders of states', since our fathers performed these heroic deeds before us. 'Our proper business is improvement', he said – and then, in a neat epistrophe (or repetition of a word or words at the end of the phrase) – 'Let our age be the age of improvement.' And so his peroration is a rising anaphora, a crescendo of commandments, each beginning with 'Let us', one of them echoing the oath to affirm a witness's truth in a court of law:

> Let us develop the resources of our land . . . Let us cultivate a true spirit of union and harmony . . . Let us extend our ideas over the whole of the vast field in which we are called to act . . . Let our object be *our country, our whole country, and nothing but our country*. And by the blessing of God may that country become a vast and splendid monument, not of oppression and terror, but of Wisdom, of Peace, and of Liberty, upon which the world may gaze with admiration forever.

Still, the present dazzles us with its progress already accomplished: 'A day of peace has at length succeeded; and now that the strife has subsided, and the smoke cleared away, we may begin to see what has actually been done, permanently changing the state and condition of human society.' Barriers of nationality and distance are melting away: 'Knowledge has, in our time, triumphed, and is triumphing over distance, over difference of languages, over diversity of habits, over prejudice, and over bigotry.' You can picture that optimistic anaphora acted out in a series of allegorical statues.

As a result of this new enlightenment, 'The civilized and Christian world is fast learning the great lesson, that difference of nation does not imply necessary hostility, and that all contact need not be war.' From the material base of such progress – 'mankind are not only better fed and clothed' – there grow other kinds of advancement –

'but they are able also to enjoy more leisure; they possess more refinement and more self-respect.' And it 'would require volumes' to tell of the progress made 'in the polite and the mechanic arts, and machinery and manufactures, in commerce and agriculture, in letters and in science'.

The source of all this world improvement is, apparently, the American republican, democratic revolution. Indeed, things seem to have started to get better as soon as 'the strife [had] subsided, and the smoke cleared away' of the Battle of Bunker Hill itself. Not that democratic progress was straightforward. The French Revolution, for example, 'whirled along with a fearful celerity till at length, like the chariot-wheels in the races of antiquity, it took fire from the rapidity of its own motion'. The Americans had the advantage in this respect, with – another nice (and accurate) anaphora – 'no domestic throne to overturn, no privileged orders to cast down, no violent changes of property to encounter'. All in all, though, Europe, having taken its lead from the New World, 'has come out of the contest, in which she has been so long engaged, with greatly superior knowledge, and, in many respects, a highly improved condition'.

And not just in modern Europe. The Greeks, the original instructors in the arts of democracy, now take renewed inspiration from the American democratic revolution to prosecute their prolonged war of independence from the Ottoman Empire. Democracy has caught fire in South America too: Venezuela, Columbia, Mexico, Chile, Argentina and others have established their independence from Spain and been recognized by the United States. 'If the true spark of civil and religious liberty be kindled, it will burn. Human agency cannot extinguish it.'

'We are not propagandists', Webster claims disingenuously. 'Wherever other systems are preferred . . . we leave the preference to be enjoyed.' On the other hand,

> our history hitherto proves . . . that the popular form
> is practicable . . . If in our case the representative
> system ultimately fail, popular governments must be
> pronounced impossible. No combination of circum-
> stances more favourable to the experiment can ever
> be expected to occur. The last hopes of mankind,
> therefore, rest with us . . .

As a patriotic New Englander Webster would have known John Winthrop's sermon on the *Arbella* (discussed in chapter Two) as a call for the colonists of Massachusetts Bay to make their community a 'city on a hill' for others to emulate. Not until the presidency of John F. Kennedy would the tide of American exceptionalism flood again so high.

> How long ago was it? Eighty or so years since, upon
> the Fourth day of July, for the first time in the world, a
> union body of representatives was assembled to declare
> as a self-evident truth that all men were created equal.

There is something wrong here, surely? This reads like one of those spoof 'First Drafts' in *Private Eye*. In fact, it was part of an unprepared speech that President Abraham Lincoln gave from a window of the White House on

7 July 1863 to hundreds of people gathered to celebrate the Union forces' capture of Vicksburg, Mississippi.

Just to be clear, this is what an impromptu speech by Abraham Lincoln sounds like. Set alongside the beginning of the Gettysburg Address, with its sonorous 'Four score and seven years ago', a style of dating drawn from the Bible and also *Macbeth*, Lincoln's favourite Shakespeare play, it should be enough to dispel what Garry Wills calls the 'silly but persistent myth' that Lincoln had jotted down the later speech on the back of an envelope on the train to Gettysburg, or even thought it up during the ceremony to dedicate the battlefield.[2]

Gettysburg, Pennsylvania, was the site of another battle, but a vastly more murderous one than Bunker Hill. Over 51,000 were killed between 1 and 3 July 1863 – 28,063 Confederate soldiers and 23,049 Union. To put it into perspective, that is nearly as many American deaths in battle as happened during the whole Vietnam War.[3] Or to visualize the scale of slaughter, just think of the names it took to fill the 246-ft-long wall that makes up Maya Lin's Vietnam War Memorial alongside the National Mall in Washington.

For all the killing, the battle had hardly proved decisive. Though the Union forces stopped the Confederates' invasion of the north in its tracks, they failed to follow the enemy's retreat, allowing Lee, the Confederate commander, eventually to get what was left of his army across the flooded Potomac River into Virginia.

After the battle the dead horses were burned and the human corpses buried haphazardly and shallowly. At length a contractor was found to rebury the bodies and a 'rural architect' engaged to lay out 17 acres, with the graves arranged in great curving ranks on a graded incline.[4] The cemetery was opened on 19 November 1863. Lincoln's role was to utter 'a few appropriate remarks' following the main observances, formally to conclude the proceedings and to dedicate the cemetery. The main event, the original 'Gettysburg Address' in the contemporary publicity, was to be delivered by another orating heavyweight from Massachusetts. This was Edward Everett, who, like his friend Webster, had served in the House and Senate and as U.S. secretary of state, but also as governor of Massachusetts, United States minister to Great Britain and – just for good measure – president of Harvard.

Everett's two-hour history of the events leading up to the Civil War, his detailed account and analysis of the war itself – all set in the historical context of civil strife in England, Germany, Italy and France – took him two months to research and write. In fact, the opening of the cemetery had to be delayed to accommodate his preparation. His speech was widely admired when published. Today it reads well, and by all accounts, since audiences in those days relished long speeches as a mark of serious commitment, it was well received. Lincoln's brief follow-on was neither expected to be nor received as a rousing work of oratory, but as the solemn 'Dedicatory Remarks', as they were described in the official pro-gramme. Even so, and brief as it was, it was interrupted by applause five times.

In *Lincoln at Gettysburg*, his masterpiece of historical contextualization, Garry Wills shows the debt of both

speakers to the romantic revaluation of fifth-century
Athens as the fountainhead of democracy, and particularly
to the set piece of Athenian public oratory, the *epitaphios*,
or funeral address, as perfected by the great general
and statesman Pericles in his speech over the ashes
of Athenians who had fallen in the first year of the
Peloponnesian War. At the outset of his own speech
Everett refers explicitly to this tradition.

The main rhetorical features of the *epitaphios* are
that the orator speaks in the plural, as the voice of the
citizenry as a whole; he refers to the dead, not by name,
but as 'these [men]', as representative of all who died; he
uses antithesis to contrast the living and the dead, word
and deed, teachers and taught, Athens and other city
states. As a whole, the Greek funeral speech was divided
between praise for the fallen (*epainesis*) and the lesson
that their sacrifice teaches the living (*parainesis*).

Both Everett and Lincoln wanted to enfold the
American instance within this great classical tradition –
not just to add the glamour of antiquity but because the
convention offered a grammar to enforce the sense of a
community coming together. So Lincoln too uses the
plural 'we', and further generalizes the occasion and what
it means: 'a great civil war', not just this war; 'a great
battlefield', not just this battlefield; 'any nation so
conceived', not just the United States.

He refers to 'these dead', not by name or regiment.
His contrasts include the living and dead, of course –
'the brave men, living and dead' – but also word and deed
in 'what we say here ... what they did here' and (as Wills
puts it) 'separates America from other nations [including

Athens, it should be noted] by its birth from a proposition': that all men are created equal. He also observes the main headings of praise of the dead and lessons for the living: 'It is for the living, rather, to be dedicated to the unfinished work . . .'.[5]

Compared to almost any sentence plucked at random from Webster's Bunker Hill speech, Lincoln's seems a triumph of the plain style. Here is Webster: 'And now let us indulge an honest exultation in the conviction of the benefit which the example of our country has pro-duced and is likely to produce on human freedom and human happiness.' He is saying that Americans rejoice in the example their country has set for the rest of the world, but he hides this clear statement in a string of abstractions set in prepositional phrases. Where is the main verb in all this? Strictly analysed, it is 'Let' – and that is further obscured by being set in the optative mood. The real business, what he really wants to say, is all buried in relative clauses.

In his preference for active verbs taking direct objects Lincoln's expression is far clearer than Webster's. But plain? Not always in the commonly accepted journalistic sense. 'Fourscore and seven' seems an unduly fancy way of saying 87. And what about 'conceived', 'proposition', 'consecrate' and 'hallow'? Then there is the frequent repetition of words and phrases, which a journalist would alleviate by elegant variation, like 'Monarch' and 'His Majesty' standing in for 'King,' or 'Pontiff' for 'Pope': 'great battlefield . . . that field'; 'these honored dead . . . these dead'; 'of the people, by the people, for the people'.

In places the repetition is insistent: 'conceived in liberty and dedicated'; 'so conceived and so dedicated'; 'we have come to dedicate'; 'we cannot dedicate'; 'It is for us the living rather to be dedicated here'; 'It is rather for us to be here dedicated'.

But consider how well these breaches of journalistic convention work. 'Fourscore', reminding his hearers of Psalm 90 – 'The days of our life are threescore years and ten' – announces from the start that this is to be a statement set apart from ordinary speech. Compare the 'eighty or so years' at the start of his impromptu remarks on 7 July. 'Hallow' and 'consecrate' reinforce that sense, fixing its special nature as a quasi-religious discourse. This is the oratory of civil religion again, but this time set to a tone far more sombre than Webster's breezy optimism.

'Conceived' is there for a purpose too. It is part of the only extended metaphor in the speech, a figurative line beginning with 'fathers brought forth', then running through 'new birth' to 'not perish'. It sets American history in the wider, more elemental context of irresistible natural processes: conception, birth and death. Out of death on this battlefield will come a 'new birth of freedom'. The tone and paraphraseable content are tentative, hopeful rather than certain, but the metaphor makes it as inevitable as in any natural process.

'Proposition' denotes a scientific hypothesis. Now this war is 'testing', as in a scientific experiment, whether 'that nation or any nation so conceived and so dedicated can long endure'. The democratic project had long seemed precarious – remember that Jefferson acknowledged that 'some honest men fear that a Republican government can not be strong', before exhorting his audience 'with courage and confidence [to] pursue our own Federal and Republican principles'. Webster too, for all his optimism, needed to affirm that 'our history hitherto proves ... that the popular form is practicable'.

But for Lincoln the adversary was more starkly demarcated. It was the slave-holding South that challenged the 'proposition that all men are created equal'. So the war is 'testing' whether the South is strong enough to undermine and defeat the democratic union. And as an experience for all those involved in it, Union as well as Confederate, it was a 'test' in another sense too: a rite of passage into a 'new birth of freedom', which, if the north were victorious, would include emancipation of the slaves. The Emancipation Proclamation had become law on 1 January of that year.

As for those repetitions, consider this: 'It is for us the living rather to be dedicated here ... It is rather for us to be here dedicated.' If this were a literary manuscript, a scholar might suspect an uncancelled emendation. A journalist might consider this degree of duplication a waste of space. But what might look redundant in a printed text can be the very heartbeat of a public speech. It works as a means of emphasis, a sort of repeated drum roll announcing the crucial message of the address: that we still have unfinished work to do.

The function of repetition in spoken address is even more powerful in that seemingly almost obsessive reiteration of 'conceived in liberty and dedicated' (line 2), 'conceived and so dedicated' (lines 3–4), 'a great battlefield' (line 4), 'dedicate a portion of that field' (line 5), 'we

cannot dedicate, we cannot consecrate, we cannot hallow'
(line 7), 'the brave men, living and dead . . . have
consecrated (line 8), 'it is for us . . . to be dedicated' (line
10), 'it is rather for us to be dedicated' (lines 11– 12),
'these honored dead' (line 12), 'these dead' (line 14).

These repetitions stand out particularly because, as
Wills shows, Lincoln continues to use the antecedent
nouns like '[battle]field' and 'these honored dead' instead
of substituting for them pronouns like 'it' or 'they' on
second and subsequent mention. 'This linking up by
explicit repetition', Wills writes, 'amounts to a kind
of hook-and-eye method for joining the parts of his
address.'[6] Once again, it is not so much how the speech
looks as how it sounds.

Besides, these words are not simply repeated. When
'we' do it, 'consecrate' is ceremonial; when 'the brave
men, living and dead' do it, it becomes something deeper
and more elemental. 'Dedicated' goes from meaning
'committed' (lines 1, 4) to 'set aside' (lines 5, 7), to 'pledge',
'obligate' or even 'devote' (lines 10, 13). Each fresh
occurrence adds meaning, while enriched by the history
of its former uses.

For the famous and moving triadic epistrophe that
closes the speech, at least two sources have been
suggested. One is Webster's Second Reply to Robert Y.
Hayne of South Carolina, in a Senate debate over the
relative power of the Federal Government and that of
the states. Webster argued that the former should take
precedence, because 'It is, Sir, the people's Constitution,
the people's government, made for the people, made by
the people, and answerable to the people.'

The other, suggested by Wills, is the transcendentalist Unitarian and abolitionist Theodore Parker extolling the Declaration of Independence as 'The American Idea', an idea 'that demands for its organization a democracy – a government of all, for all, by all'.[7]

For Webster, the Constitution, which made up the Ten Commandments in his civic religion, was the vehicle that carried the original impulse of the people's revolution, but according to Garry Wills, the people had a grittier historical reality for Webster than for Parker. For Webster 'the term meant . . . the *one* people that brought itself into being while issuing the Declaration'.[8] For Lincoln too the true object of devotion, the moment the idea of America was founded, was neither the Revolutionary War nor the drafting of the Constitution – the work of Webster's fighters and framers – but the event that had preceded both of these, the Declaration of Independence.

The immediate cause of this renewed attention to the Declaration was the endless squabbling between the North and the South over what the Constitution said, or didn't say, about slavery. In debating the four bills finally passed as the Compromise of 1850, which settled the issue of whether territories captured during the Mexican–American War should be admitted as slave-holding or free states, Senator William H. Seward argued that 'a higher law' than the Constitution condemned slavery, the law of morality.[9]

It was that law, above all, that Lincoln found enshrined in the Declaration, 'the proposition that all men are created equal'. That was the true foundation of the truly new nation. Compared to the Declaration, the

Constitution was a later accretion of specificities, the engineering, more or less efficacious, of the original invention.

This imaginative leap back over intervening complications to the original purity of intention is a very Protestant argument. Perhaps that accounts in part for the more or less immediate impact of the Gettysburg Address and its perennial appeal. This is the secular equivalent of the Reformation itself, the impulse to clear away the complexity and corruption of Catholic doctrine and ritual, in order to get back to the simple faith of the early Christian Church. It is Lincoln's own oratory of civil religion.

The other reason for the urgent appeal of the Gettysburg Address is that for Lincoln, unlike Webster, there is no easy division of American generations into fighters and framers, defenders and developers. Here we are all (either directly or by proxy) fighters in this 'great civil war', defenders, developers and founders again, since we are acting as midwives to a 'new birth of freedom'. As Wills puts it, 'The "great task remaining" at the end of his Address is not something inferior to the great deeds of the fathers. It is the same work, always being done.'[10]

Abraham Lincoln was assassinated on 15 April 1865, just five days after the Civil War ended. In his eulogy on the dead president, Senator Charles Sumner called the Gettysburg Address a 'monumental act'. He said Lincoln was wrong to say that 'the world will little note, nor long remember what we say here'. Rather, 'The world noted at once what he said, and will never cease to remember it. The battle itself was less important than the speech.'[11]

5

A Common Humanity:
Kennedy Confronts the Soviets

TO THIS DAY historians argue over whether John
Fitzgerald Kennedy, president from 1961 until his
assassination in November 1963, was a Cold Warrior or a
peacemaker. In fact, he was both. He came to office fully
subscribing to the Truman Doctrine that the United
States had to assume the permanent global responsibility
to lead the 'free world' – that is, the non-communist
world – in defence of 'freedom' and 'freedom-loving
peoples everywhere'. That meant supporting or installing
non-communist regimes in Europe, South America and
the Far East, even if they were autocratic and socially
reactionary. One theme of Kennedy's presidential
campaign was that the Republican administration had
'lost' Cuba to a communist revolution, as though that
country had been a u.s. possession carelessly misplaced.

Meanwhile the Soviets (as they were then called) had
raised the Cold War stakes, and American anxieties, by
testing their own hydrogen bomb in 1955. Two years later,
as if to show that they had the means of delivering that
weapon, they launched *Sputnik*, the first ever artificial
satellite to orbit the earth. In his campaign, first for the
Senate, then for the presidency, Kennedy had added a

post-*Sputnik* frightener all his own: the assertion that
his predecessor, President Dwight D. Eisenhower, had
allowed a 'missile gap' to grow between the United States
and the USSR in the latter's favour. Kennedy did not know
this to be true; the claim was pure politics. Later intelli-
gence would show that at the time the Russians had fewer
than 25 intercontinental ballistic missiles, each of which
took twenty hours to ready for launch.

Yet Kennedy also bought into the 'good-cop' branch
of U.S. Cold War strategy, the language of hope involved
in the promotion of the Marshall Plan, the rhetoric that
the real war was 'not against any country or doctrine, but
against hunger, poverty, desperation and chaos', as Senator
George C. Marshall himself had put it in his Harvard
speech of 5 June 1947. There was a much more positive
side to Kennedy's Latin America policy too, as stated in
his Inaugural Address, when he proposed his Alliance
for Progress to encourage non-communist progressive
reforms in South and Central America.

His Inaugural Address on 20 January 1961 was the
work of a number of bright young men, including the
43-year-old president himself, the youngest ever to take
that office, apart from Theodore Roosevelt. Chief among
Kennedy's legislative aides was Theodore (Ted) Sorensen,
the president's counsel and special advisor, who had
helped to write Kennedy's Pulitzer-Prize-winning *Profiles
in Courage* (1957). Another leading speechwriter was
Richard Goodwin, a young lawyer with expertise in
investigating the media. They had also sought guidance
from outside the White House. Sorensen sent out a
telegram to historians like Joseph Allan Nevins and the

economist John Kenneth Galbraith, not to mention Adlai Stevenson, the former Democratic candidate for president against Eisenhower, to get their ideas. Yet collaboration though it was, the speech reflected not just presidential policy but the contradictions within it – and not just in its overt statements but in the grain of its rhetoric.

The theme was renewal. A new politics and diplomacy were now taking over, breaking radically from the tired old comforts and compromises. Yet the old platitudes of economic and military defence were not to be abandoned. It was crucial to emphasize that the young president was not naive, but already hardened by experience. Significantly, the speech would describe this new generation as 'born in this century, tempered by war', a reminder not only of the new president's self-evident youth but also of his war heroism in saving his crew after their patrol torpedo boat had been rammed by a Japanese destroyer in August 1943. This phrase would set the keynote for the first half of Kennedy's Inaugural Address – a calculated balance between soft and hard, liberal and conservative.

Foreign relations were the priority; there were few mentions of domestic concerns. That famous 'ask not what your country can do for you – ask what you can do for your country' came in the only direct statement – not really a statement at all, rather an injunction – to 'my fellow citizens', a passage of only 265 words, or just under 19 per cent of the total of 1,400. Other entities addressed included 'every nation', 'old allies', 'peoples in the huts and villages across the globe' and 'our sister republics south of our border'.

The speech started out hard. Americans may be a new generation, it said, but they are also 'the heirs of that first revolution', the American act of independence from the mother country, and so 'unwilling to witness or permit the slow undoing of those human rights to which this nation has always been committed'. And to 'every nation . . . whether it wishes us well or ill' the new president had this message: 'We shall pay any price, bear any burden, meet any hardship, support any friend, oppose any foe, to assure the survival and the success of liberty.'

But then the tone began to soften. To the ex-colonies of Africa and Southeast Asia 'we pledge our word that one form of colonial control shall not . . . be replaced by a far more iron tyranny. We shall not always expect to find them supporting our view', he conceded, '[b]ut we shall always hope to find them strongly supporting their own freedom.'

For Latin America, out went the campaign complaint that we had 'lost' Cuba, and in came a 'special pledge – to convert our good words into a new alliance for progress – to assist free men and free governments in casting off the chains of poverty'. It was to be a sort of Marshall Plan for South and Central America. But just in case his audience thought he was offering too much, he warned, 'Let all our neighbors know that we shall join with them to oppose aggression or subversion anywhere in the Americas . . . that this Hemisphere intends to remain the master of its own house.' And so the new opening to Latin America was balanced by a reassertion of the Monroe Doctrine of 1823, that any foreign interference with states would be seen as an act of aggression, justifying u.s. intervention.

As for 'those nations who would make themselves our adversary' (note that 'make themselves' – nothing to do with America), 'we offer not a pledge but a request – that both sides begin anew to quest for peace, before the dark powers of destruction unleashed by science engulf all humanity in planned or accidental self-destruction.'

But again, the bad cop weighs in – 'We dare not tempt them with weakness. For only when our arms are sufficient beyond doubt can we be certain beyond doubt that they will never be employed' – only to be balanced again by the more reasonable 'But neither can two great and powerful groups of nations take comfort from our present course . . . both rightly alarmed by the steady spread of the deadly atom, both racing to alter that uncertain balance of terror that stays the hand of mankind's final war.'

Then this plea, in which the progressive and defensive stances are neatly telescoped within each other: 'So let us begin anew, remembering on both sides that civility is not a sign of weakness, and sincerity is always subject to proof. Let us never negotiate out of fear. But let us never fear to negotiate.' At this point, roughly halfway through, the speech turns positive and more or less stays that way, listing potential areas of agreement between the two sides of the Cold War. In four short paragraphs, each beginning 'Let both sides', it invites the United States and USSR to 'explore what problems unite us instead of belaboring those problems which divide us.' These include the 'inspection and control of arms' and bringing 'the absolute power to destroy other nations under the absolute control of all nations', the injunction to 'invoke the wonders of science instead of its terrors' and a plea to 'heed . . . the command of Isaiah – to "undo the heavy burdens . . . and let the oppressed go free"'.

So many bright young men contributing to a message so carefully balanced between progressive and established thinking meant a highly wrought speech, tightly laced by rhetorical devices. Thus we get alliteration (referring to the ex-colonies) in 'colonial control' and 'strongly supporting', and (in the passage on our adversaries), 'dark powers of destruction'. Anaphora, or repetition of the same word at the beginning of a series of sentences or clauses, functions in 'both sides overburdened . . . both rightly alarmed . . . yet both racing to alter', and in that series of paragraphs beginning 'Let both sides'. That phrase, 'free men and free governments' in the pledge to Latin America is a form of repetition of words within phrases known as conduplicatio.

Clunky metaphors also litter the text, phrases like 'the torch has been passed to a new generation', 'casting off the chains of poverty' and – this one almost extended to an allegorical scenario – 'if a beachhead of cooperation may push back the jungle of suspicion'. As for what that beachhead might lead to, it was a polysyndeton, or string of words or phrases, all linked by a conjunction, 'where the strong are just and the weak secure and the peace preserved'.

Above all, propelled by that urgent need to keep the balance between cautious convention and adventurous progress, the speech deploys figures of parallelism and antithesis: 'We shall not always expect . . . but we shall always hope' (of the newly liberated colonies); and (of any nation out there), 'whether it wishes us well or ill'.

In November 2013, on the fiftieth anniversary of Kennedy's murder, the one thing all the media remembered about him was 'Ask not what your country can do for you – ask what you can do for your country.' What made the sentence so memorable? The sentiment itself? Maybe, but it was hardly original. In *White House Ghosts*, Robert Schlesinger traces it back through President Warren G. Harding to Supreme Court Justice Oliver Wendell Holmes.[1] Maybe it was the way it was posed, that slightly arch inversion at the beginning: 'Ask not' in place of 'Do not ask'. But whatever stuck in the memory was made more vivid by the chiasmus, that criss-crossing of subject and predicate in the pattern of ABBA. In fact, so famous is the 'Ask not' formulation that it is now used as an example of chiasmus in modern guides to rhetoric like Sam Leith's *You Talkin' to Me?*[2]

Chiasmus is the keynote trope of Kennedy's First Inaugural Address. The figure, or approximations of it, like 'only when our arms are sufficient beyond doubt can we be certain beyond doubt that they will never be employed', and 'explore what problems unite us instead of belaboring those problems which divide us', pepper the speech. Apart from 'Ask not . .', the best of them, because so central to the themes of the speech and to its balanced tone, is 'Let us never negotiate out of fear. But let us never fear to negotiate.'

Chiasmus has always been associated with Sorensen, almost a signature of his authorship, but in fact the one about fearing to negotiate was suggested by J. K. Galbraith.[3] And here is an important lesson about collaboration. When all elements of a speech seem to harmonize in tone and content with the intellect and personality of the person saying the words, it doesn't really matter who first thought of them. Chiasmus was the trope of the moment because it functions as the self-reconciling antithesis; it shows the way to harmonize the opposites it proclaims. So though the rhetoric of John F. Kennedy's Inaugural Address may be a bit obtrusive, it is not merely decorative; it is a function of the underlying argument and feeling the new president wanted to project.

As he began his presidency Kennedy adhered to many of the pieties of conservative and specifically Cold War policy. The plan to invade Cuba was an overhang from the Eisenhower era, but Kennedy signed off on it. The landing at the Bay of Pigs in April 1961 was a disaster from both military and diplomatic points of view. A strong adherent to the theory of the 'domino effect' that once a foreign country 'fell' to communism, its neighbours would do the same, Kennedy supported u.s. involvement in Vietnam by increasing American troops' strength there from 500 to 16,000. On the domestic issue of civil rights in the American South, his critics allege, he was similarly defensive, underestimating the impatience of African Americans and the intransigence of white southerners.

On the other hand (so the countervailing arguments go), Kennedy did care enough about southern civil rights to federalize the state National Guard to enforce desegregation in the University of Alabama in June 1963, and his successor Lyndon Johnson's reform of black voting and other civil rights had been largely drafted during Kennedy's administration by his attorney general, his brother Robert.

And on Vietnam, the Pentagon Papers show Kennedy growing increasingly reluctant to commit further troops, commenting that like the alcoholic's first drink, it would never be enough. The papers also show that shortly before his death he approved (but did not announce) a plan to withdraw 1,000 American troops from Vietnam by the end of 1963.[4]

Kennedy's commitment to the Cold War met its severest test in the Cuban missile crisis. In October 1962 American spy planes discovered that the Soviets were installing missiles in Cuba capable of delivering nuclear weapons to the U.S. Rejecting advice from his military advisors to bomb Cuba forthwith, Kennedy set up a naval blockade of the island while demanding the removal of the weapons. Eventually the Russians agreed, after Kennedy promised never again to invade Cuba, and – secretly – to remove similar American missiles from Turkey.

The Cuban missile crisis caused Kennedy to reconsider his Cold War convictions. In the words of the historian Philip Foner, 'He appears to have been shocked by the casual way military leaders spoke of "winning" a nuclear exchange in which tens of millions of Americans and Russians were certain to die.'[5] It was time for some kind of rapprochement, and following their behind-the-scenes negotiations during the course of the Cuban missile crisis both Kennedy and Khrushchev were anxious to explore further modes of cooperation.

Throughout the 1950s there had been tentative exchanges between the Soviet Union and the United States over various kinds of arms control, ranging from

complete disarmament to a partial test ban of nuclear
weapons – partial because it excluded underground tests.
Two months after the missile crisis Khrushchev wrote to
Kennedy to say that 'the time has come now to put an end
once and for all to nuclear tests.' In April 1963 Kennedy
sent a message to Khrushchev via the editor of the
Saturday Review, Norman Cousins, who was travelling in
the Soviet Union at the time, saying that he wanted to
re-start nuclear test-ban negotiations. The message came
back that the premier was willing to talk, but that he
considered the next move to be up to the president.

Kennedy's move came in a commencement address
delivered to the graduating class of American University,
delivered outdoors on a sunny campus in Washington, DC,
on 10 June 1963. Drafted mainly by Sorensen, the speech
incorporated ideas circulating between the president
himself, Cousins, national security advisor McGeorge
Bundy, the historian Arthur Schlesinger Jr, and Walt
Rostow, chairman of the State Department's Policy
Planning Council. Not involved at this stage were
secretary of state Dean Rusk or secretary of defense
Robert McNamara. The White House team did not
want the speech to get entangled with the State or
Defense Department bureaucracy attempting to enforce
their entrenched Cold War positions.[6]

The Commencement Address was more expansive
than the Inaugural. It was longer – nearly 3,500 words
as against 1,900 – and its range of reference widened in
space and time, to 'not merely peace for Americans but
peace for all men and women – not merely peace in our
time but peace for all time'. The vast destructive power

of the stockpiled nuclear weapons on both sides of the Cold War made peace an especially urgent project, especially 'when the deadly poisons produced by a nuclear exchange would be carried by wind and water and soil and seed to the far corners of the globe and to generations yet unborn'.

Yet for all its universalizing, the speech concentrated on particulars, the first practical steps that could be taken to bring about peace. 'World peace' here is not the vague aspiration of a Miss World candidate. 'I am not referring to the absolute, infinite concept of peace and goodwill of which some fantasies and fanatics dream', he said. 'Let us focus instead on a more practical, more attainable peace – based not on a sudden revolution in human nature but on a gradual evolution in human institutions.'

To help his audience conceptualize this process Kennedy used the smaller models of family and local communities. With the world at peace, he said, 'There will still be quarrels and conflicting interests, as there are within families and nations.' Like peace in the community, world peace 'does not require that each man love his neighbor – it requires only that they live together in mutual tolerance, submitting their disputes to a just and peaceful settlement'.

To limit the idea of peace to its practical realities, to break the concept down to its concrete possibilities is to guard against a dangerous pessimism. When the image of peace is abstract and ill defined, the result is that

Too many of us think it is impossible. Too many think it unreal. But that is a dangerous, defeatist belief. It

leads to the conclusion that war is inevitable – that
mankind is doomed – that we are gripped by forces
we cannot control.

The antidote to such pessimism is belief in human agency,
in the historical process as evolving in human institutions.

So what are these practical steps to peace? First, 'Let
us also direct our attention to our common interests.'
Second, 'Nuclear powers must avert those confrontations
which bring an adversary to a choice of either a humiliat-
ing retreat or a nuclear war.' Third, while continuing to
negotiate in Geneva about arms control and – ultimately
– 'general and complete disarmament', let us take
the first practical step of agreeing a 'treaty to outlaw
nuclear tests'.

At this point, in the eighteenth minute of a speech
lasting for 23, Kennedy announced 'two important
decisions'. First, he would go to Moscow to meet with
Khrushchev and British Prime Minister Harold
Macmillan, then representing the other two nuclear
powers, to begin talks on a comprehensive test ban treaty
(audience applause). Second, and in the meantime, he
would impose a unilateral ban on u.s. tests in the
atmosphere so long as other states complied (again,
applause – and it did not come that often during this
speech).

The more optimistic content is wrapped in a more
expansive rhetoric. In place of the contrasting, to and fro
chiasmus so characteristic of the Inaugural Address, here
the leading figure is anaphora:

Total war makes no sense in an age when great powers
. . . refuse to surrender without resort to [nuclear]
forces. It makes no sense in an age when a single
nuclear weapon contains almost ten times the explosive
force delivered by all the allied air forces in the Second
World War. It makes no sense in an age when the
deadly poisons produced by a nuclear exchange would
be carried by wind and water and soil and seed to the
far corners of the globe and to generations yet unborn.

And again, following his announcement of America's
unilateral test ban, he returned to the definition of peace:

And is not peace, in the last analysis, basically a matter
of human rights – the right to live out our lives
without fear of devastation – the right to breathe air
as nature provided it – the right of future generations
to a healthy existence?

So while in the Inaugural Address Kennedy needed to
establish the balance between the bad and good cop, here
in the American University Commencement Address he
could deploy the figure of repetition and accumulation,
freeing up the prose rhythm to add momentum to a
promise for the future.

'Promise' was a word much used in the media on the
50th anniversary of Kennedy's assassination. The
consensus was that although he did not achieve much of
substance in the (admittedly meagre) 1,036 days allotted
to his presidency, he promised much. He inspired hope
for the future. 'It would, forever, be a story of what might

have been', as Jonathan Freedland wrote in *The Guardian* for 22 November 2013, 'of potential snuffed out before its time.'

But that hope itself was a crowning achievement. To understand why, you have to recall, or ask someone old enough to know, what it felt like to live in the American 1950s – the thousand ways the Cold War was numbing the public sphere: the rampant propaganda of the John Birch Society; the House Un-American Activities Committee subpoenaing liberal actors and writers; Senator Joe McCarthy's Senate Permanent Subcommittee on Investigations targeting left-wingers and homosexuals in government public service; 'loyalty oaths' in the state universities and other public services – and all this made politically acceptable by the universal anxiety triggered by the constant dread of nuclear war.

Listen to what Kennedy says in the speech. 'No government or social system is so evil that its people must be considered as lacking in virtue.' He meant the Soviets. And again: 'We can still hail the Russian people for their many achievements – in science and space, in economic and industrial growth, in culture and in acts of courage.' The U.S. and Russia have never fought each other. The Soviets hate war as much as Americans do. And no wonder, since: 'No nation in the history of battle ever suffered more than the Soviet Union suffered in the course of the Second World War. At least 20 million lost their lives. Countless millions of homes and farms were burned or sacked. A third of the nation's territory, including nearly two thirds of its industrial base, was turned into a wasteland.' And in the last analysis, 'We all breathe the same air. We all cherish our children's future. And we are all mortal.'

'Viewed from the twenty-first century', writes Robert Schlesinger, 'this elegant rhetoric hardly seems revolutionary, but at the time it was the kind of speech that only a proven Cold Warrior could successfully give without seeming weak in the face of the Communist threat.'[7] And although the initial response in the United States was muted (in Europe and especially the Soviet Union the speech was highly praised), the Partial Test Ban Treaty signed in October 1963, as the first practical step to peace, really did begin to disperse that corrosive atmosphere.

6

Unity and the Union:
Lincoln and Martin Luther King Jr

E PLURIBUS UNUM, the motto on the ribbon clenched in
the eagle's bill on the Great Seal of the United States, can
still be realized: one out of many, and all created equal.
Above all the greatest Great American Speeches advance
the hope of unity – of class, of race, of the Federal Union
itself.

Though inaugural addresses often pose as pivotal
points in the nation's history, few have been delivered at a
moment of actual national crisis. At his first inaugural on
4 March 1933 Franklin Delano Roosevelt had to confront
the depths of the Great Depression, when American
industrial production had fallen by 45 per cent, farm
prices were down by 60 per cent and one in four of the
working population was out of a job. When Abraham
Lincoln took the oath on Monday, 4 March 1861, the
country wasn't just depressed; it was falling apart.

Abraham Lincoln had won the presidential election
for the Republican party in November 1860, against a
divided opposition consisting of northern Democrats,
southern Democrats and the newly formed
Constitutional Party. Though winning less than 40 per
cent of the popular ballot, he had managed to accumulate

180 of the 203 electoral votes, mainly from the populous states in the north and east, plus California and Oregon. He had no support whatever from the southern slave-holding states.

The South was devastated. Fearing the federal government would eventually abolish slavery and thus destroy their plantation economy, and sensing that the growing population and economic power of the north would render the South increasingly irrelevant to the nation's political processes, they resolved to leave the Union. In the wake of Lincoln's election seven of the southern states seceded immediately. Others would follow. Just two weeks before Lincoln took the oath, Jefferson Davis was inaugurated as president of the self-styled Confederate States of America.

Lincoln had travelled to Washington from his family home in Springfield, Illinois, taking in a number of northern states on the way, where he met people and gave speeches. So heated had the secession issue become that as he approached Maryland, a slave-holding state still in the Union, though with popular support for the Confederacy, an assassination threat forced him to travel through Baltimore on a special train in the middle of the night. From there he went to Washington by a secret route, guarded by General Winfield Scott's soldiers.

On the day of his inauguration, however, despite the danger, the president-elect rode to the Capitol in an open carriage alongside the outgoing president, James Buchanan, to take the oath of office. In his first Inaugural Address there was no time or space for the usual pleasantries or promises: no occasion for Adams's guarded praise for the new Constitution and pious hopes for the future of his young country; no hope of Jefferson's search for common ground between opposing parties; none of the foreign affairs to which Kennedy would later draw the country's attention. Indeed, Lincoln said as much, beginning his Inaugural Address with a negative: 'I do not consider it necessary at present for me to discuss those matters of administration about which there is no special anxiety or excitement.'

What he did need to do, urgently, was to placate the South and warn against the anarchy of secession. This he would attempt in three phases. First, he reminded his audience that he had never been an abolitionist, never threatened to interfere with slavery in the South (though he had been campaigning for six years against the extension of slavery in the newly settled territories). Then he questioned whether anyone could in logic or legality secede from the Union. Finally he appealed to the better nature of his fellow citizens.

So he began by reassuring the South that 'their property, and their peace, and personal security' were safe under his presidency, citing his own former speeches to show that he had 'no purpose, directly or indirectly, to interfere with the institution of slavery in the States where it exists'.

He then moved on to the Constitution, that much combed-over document that the South thought justified slavery, and sought to amend where it did not. And here the speech moves with a relentless logic seldom found in the public oratory of whatever nation. Lincoln's argument went as follows. The United States, in the form of the Constitution, is either 'a government proper' or 'an

association of States in the nature of a contract merely'.
If it is a government proper, then it is perpetual, for what
'government ever had a provision in its organic law for its
own termination'? If the Constitution is only a contract
between the parties of the States, 'can it . . . be peaceably
unmade by less than all the parties who made it?'

Under this question of the Constitution lay a deeper
truth, since what was at issue was nothing less than the
existence of the Union itself. 'The Union is much older
than the Constitution', Lincoln argued. Its lineage runs
back through the Articles of Confederation in 1778 to
the Declaration of Independence which, as we have seen
in chapter Four and as Wills points out, 'to Lincoln and
Webster . . . was closer to being *the* founding document
of the United States than was the Constitution'.[1] As for
the Constitution, as Lincoln concluded this phase of the
argument, one of its objectives was 'to form a more perfect
Union'. The idea of a 'perfect Union' is the keystone of
Lincoln's proof: 'But if destruction of the Union by one or
by a part only of the States be lawfully possible, the Union
is *less* perfect than before the Constitution, having lost the
vital element of perpetuity.' This is a distant echo of the
ontological proof of God, first advanced by St Anselm
of Canterbury in 1078. If it is possible to imagine a being
than which no greater can be conceived, then that being
must exist, since a being that existed in the mind only and
not in actuality would be less great than greatest. Lincoln's
Union, pre-existing, then motivating and in turn con-
firmed by the Constitution, is perfect; therefore 'it follows
. . . that no State upon its own mere motion can lawfully
get out of the Union'.

There is more to follow in this course in civics for a South apparently forgetful of the basic workings of American democracy. First, the Constitution could never provide a ruling specific to every eventuality. This lesson he hammers home with a fine epistrophe:

> Shall fugitives from labor be surrendered by national or by State authority? The Constitution does not expressly say. *May* Congress prohibit slavery in the Territories? The Constitution does not expressly say. *Must* Congress protect slavery in the Territories? The Constitution does not expressly say.

Second, there will always be a majority for and a minority against any policy, but the 'majority is held in restraint by constitutional checks and limitations', and will always wax and wane in response to popular opinion. And popular opinion is 'the only true sovereign of a free people'. It follows, then, that for the disappointed minority simply to secede at any one given point in this process would be entirely foreign to American democracy. Besides, once the precedent is set, 'a minority of their own will secede from them whenever a majority refuses to be controlled by such minority', and so on, *ad infinitum.*

Then consider how secession will change our status. We will become aliens not friends; the choice of 'alien', rather than the more-to-be-expected 'enemy', makes the contrast especially stark. 'Can aliens make treaties easier than friends can make laws? Can treaties be more faith-fully enforced between aliens, than laws can among friends?' Here, where the rhetoric shifts from classical dispute to biblical distich – that characteristic parallel statement in different wording – Lincoln's tone turns from the didactic to that of the third phase of his inaugural, the appeal. 'Why should there not be a patient confidence in the ultimate justice of the people?' he asked, almost plaintively.

His closing paragraph is his most poignant, and also most powerful. For this his secretary of state, William Seward, had offered a draft. What Lincoln did with it provides a fascinating insight into what Wills calls his 'verbal workshop'.[2] Here is the start of Seward's draft:

> I close.
>   We are not, we must not be aliens or enemies, but fellow-countrymen and brethren.

And here is Lincoln's:

> I am loth to close.
>   We are not enemies, but friends. We must not be enemies.

Lincoln wants to seem unwilling to close, so urgent is the situation and his message to its clarification. Seward is anxious to avoid repetition, so he dresses the sentiment up with elegant variation. As in the Gettysburg Address, Lincoln does not run from repetition, but deploys it, in this case as part of a rhetorical device known as diacope, to emphasize the unthinkability of fellow citizens becoming enemies.

Seward's closing paragraph tries ambitiously for an extended metaphor that unites the nation in the threat of its dissolution:

> The mystic chords which, proceeding from so many battle-fields and so many patriot graves, pass through all the hearts and all the hearths in this broad continent of ours, will yet harmonize in their ancient music when breathed upon by the guardian angels of the nation.

And look what Lincoln did with that:

> The mystic chords of memory, stretching from every battlefield and patriot grave, to every living heart and hearthstone, all over this broad land, will yet swell the chorus of the Union, when again touched, as surely they will be, by the better angels of our nature.

Wills explains that these 'chords' are not musical sounds but 'cords', that Lincoln spelled the two words inter-changeably. Seward's elaborate conceit seems to go something like this: invisible and mysterious strings connect the hearts and hearths of every American to the sacrifices made by our forebears. When the 'guardian angels' of our nation breathe upon these strings, they will tremble as a kind of Aeolian harp in the breeze coming in through an open window, reawakening the ancient harmonics that unite the nation.

Lincoln works with the same image, while shortening it and making it less prolix. Seward's 'mystic chords which, proceeding from', for example, becomes Lincoln's 'mystic chords of memory'. But he also takes it further, with his pun on 'chords' as strings and as lines on a circle or sphere. 'He uses the geometric term for a line across a circle's arc', writes Wills, 'as the chord on a tortoise shell gave Orpheus his lute'.[3]

But Lincoln's really profound revision was to change Seward's 'the guardian angels of the nation' into 'the better angels of our nature'. Just who and where are Seward's 'guardian angels'? They are a pious hope, like those statues in New England cemeteries pointing to the sky as though to indicate where to look for the departed. Lincoln's better angels, though based on that old emblem that each of us has a good and bad angel sitting on opposite shoulders, nevertheless expresses the reality that we can choose, as individuals.

These angels really exist in the form of our impulses and inclinations, and can, through our agency, really interact with real events. The Union will be saved, not through the intervention of some unlikely *deus ex machina*, but through ourselves, however mighty or humble. Fred Kaplan, who also admires Lincoln's revision, adds the crucial point that it draws on that Protestant belief in individual moral choice, 'directing responsibility for the national condition . . . to the fact that human nature contained both good and evil'.[4]

The last of our addresses by prominent public figures is the most complete example of the Great American Speech. First of all, it is both figuratively and literally monumental – figuratively in the sense that it has become

a landmark standing for a great campaign, and literally
in two senses. First, it was delivered at the portal of the
Lincoln Memorial, through which, behind the speakers'
podium, the television and still pictures showed the huge
stature of the seated emancipator, lit from within the
building. Second, its telling sentence 'With this faith
we will be able to hew out of the mountain of despair a
stone of hope' is inscribed on the Martin Luther King Jr
Memorial, southwest of Washington's National Mall, and
gave sculptor, Lei Yixin, the idea to design the monument
as if the man were emerging from a block of stone.

Again, the speech appealed to 'the better angels of
our nature', since, although it argued passionately for the
rights of a disadvantaged race, it did so within the context
of greater unity and equality for all classes and conditions
of Americans.

And finally, it belongs unambiguously to the genre
of the spoken word, since much of its effect depends on
rhythm and pitch, and the audience reaction can be heard
both to prompt and to respond to the speaker's voice.
King's speech was, in effect, a sermon. 'A sermon is not
an essay to be read, but a discourse to be heard', King had
written in a book of his sermons published that year.[5]

The occasion was, of course, the great March on
Washington for Jobs and Freedom. On 28 August 1963
nearly 250,000 Americans – 190,000 of them black and
60,000 white – had arrived by chartered buses and trains
from all over the country to surround the long reflecting
pool between the Washington and Lincoln monuments,
and to listen to songs and speeches from the leaders and
sympathizers of the massive campaign for African

American civil rights. In addition to ordinary citizens, black and white, with their picnic baskets, water jugs and Bibles, actors, musicians and other celebrities joined the crowd, among them Josephine Baker, Harry Belafonte, Paul Newman, Charlton Heston, Sidney Poitier, Sammy Davis Jr, Burt Lancaster, James Garner and Marlon Brando.

This was not the first march on Washington to be planned by African American campaigners. The civil rights activist Bayard Rustin and the black labour leader A. Philip Randolph, president of the Brotherhood of Sleeping Car Porters, first threatened to march on Washington in 1941, until President Roosevelt issued an Executive Order prohibiting discrimination against hiring blacks in the defence industries.

Over twenty years later the two got together to organize a much larger march with a wider range of campaign goals, including the immediate passage of civil rights legislation, an end to discrimination in hiring for publically funded jobs, a programme of public works and minimum wage of $2 per hour across the country. Now a younger generation was also involved, in the form of the Student Nonviolent Coordinating Committee (SNCC), along with the more long-standing campaigners, the National Association for the Advancement of Colored People (NAACP), together with labour unions like the United Auto Workers and church groups like the Southern Christian Leadership Conference, headed by Martin Luther King Jr.

The march came at the end of a decade of increasingly intense struggle for civil rights. After the Supreme Court

ruled in 1954 that 'equal but separate' education of white
and black students in public schools and colleges might
be separate but certainly wasn't equal,[6] the whole structure
of segregation began to break down, causing a vehement
and sometimes violent reaction among many white southerners. The next issue to be challenged was segregation on
public transport, when on 1 December 1955 Rosa Parks
refused to give up her seat in the white section of a bus in
Montgomery, Alabama, thus prompting a year-long black
boycott of the city's buses before the city backed down.
Attempts by the SNCC in 1962 to promote the registration
of black voters met with violent resistance. Many activists
were beaten up and one, Herbert Lee, was murdered.

The most immediate impulse behind the March
on Washington was a speech President Kennedy gave
on radio and television on the night of 11 July 1963,
alerting the nation to its moral obligation to pass a
Civil Rights Act 'giving all Americans the right to be
served in facilities which are open to the public – hotels,
restaurants, theaters, retail stores, and similar establish-
ments', as well as 'greater protection for the right to vote'.
'One hundred years . . . have passed', he said,

> since President Lincoln freed the slaves, yet their heirs
> . . . are not fully free. They are not yet freed from the
> bonds of injustice . . . this Nation . . . will not be fully
> free until all its citizens are free . . . Now the time has
> come for this Nation to fulfil its promise.

Despite this crucial policy initiative, Kennedy himself was
anxious about the march, wary of what he anticipated as a

protest movement in the nation's capital, but once the organizers assured him that they would be cooperating with the Washington police, and that no sit-ins or other acts of civil disobedience would be allowed, he gave the march his blessing.

The event was studiously ecumenical and multi-racial. Religious contributions came from a Protestant minister, a rabbi and the Catholic Archbishop of Washington, who intoned the invocation. Main speakers included the organizers of the march – Randolph and Rustin, of course, but also John Lewis, chairman of the SNCC, Floyd McKissick of the Council for Racial Equality and Roy Wilkins from the NAACP – and labour leader Walter Reuther. Music came from gospel singer Mahalia Jackson, the classical contralto Marion Anderson and the folk artists Joan Baez and Bob Dylan, not to mention Peter, Paul and Mary, who performed the old Weavers favourite, 'If I Had a Hammer'.

Martin Luther King Jr had agreed to speak right at the end, by which time the organizers expected most people to be heading back to their chartered buses and trains. It didn't turn out that way. The audience stayed put, and heard every one of the 1,756 words that, above all, have put the March on Washington on the historical map.

There had been a good deal of debate among King and his advisors about what kind of speech he should give. Rustin had wanted something about labour in it. Others had wanted it to be more like one of his church sermons. 'Martin, you have to preach', said the Reverend Ralph Abernathy, King's close friend and colleague in the Southern Christian Leadership Conference. 'Most of the folks coming tomorrow are coming to hear you preach.'

The 'I have a dream' motif was already well known. King had worked the same theme into speeches in Detroit and Chicago that year. Should it be used again? Wyatt Walker, who helped him prepare the speech the night before in Washington's Willard Hotel, thought not. 'Don't use the lines about "I have a dream"', he said. 'It's cliché.' When at four in the morning King handed over the draft to be printed and distributed, 'I have a dream' was not part of it.[7]

The bulk of King's speech took its lead from Kennedy's argument that 100 years after Lincoln's Emancipation Proclamation, the descendants of those slaves were still not wholly free. Standing in front of the Lincoln Memorial and using that same sonorous notation of historical time that began the Gettysburg Address, King made sure of the connection:

> Five score years ago, a great American, in whose symbolic shadow we stand today, signed the Emancipation Proclamation . . . But one hundred years later, the Negro is still not free. One hundred years later, the life of the Negro is still sadly crippled by the manacles of segregation and the chains of discrimination. One hundred years later, the Negro lives on a lonely island of poverty in the midst of a vast ocean of material prosperity. One hundred years later, the Negro is still languished in the corners of American society and finds himself in exile in his own land.

There is nothing subtle about the rhetoric here. The insistent anaphorae of 'One hundred years later' – and later in the speech the repeated 'Now is the time' and 'We can never be satisfied' – read as hectoring. Yet when heard, as it can be on dozens of online recordings, these phrases come over almost as liturgical, and any threat of rhythmic monotony is dispelled by his varied emphases and occasional elisions with the word following, such as the run-on between 'prosperity' and with the first word of the (final) 'One hundred years', or the heavy stress on 'not' in the last of the 'not-satisfied' anaphorae: 'No, no, we are not satisfied, and we will NOT be satisfied.'

Equally traditional as his repetitive phrasing is King's use of that old Protestant reformation strategy of the retrospective revolution. Just as the elaborate ceremonies, architecture, hierarchies and liturgical complexity of the Roman Catholic Church should be reformed by reverting to the candour of the early church, where believers met in each other's houses; just as Lincoln's first Inaugural and the Gettysburg Address taught that American present discord could be resolved when their better angels turned back for guidance to the Declaration of Independence; so Martin Luther King Jr imagined the Declaration as a 'promissory note', a guarantee 'that all men, yes, black men as well as white men, would be guaranteed the unalienable rights of life, liberty, and the pursuit of happiness'.

For African Americans, though, that note had turned out to be a 'bad check, a check which has come back marked "insufficient funds"'. Laughter and prolonged applause at this point shows just how much his audience appreciated that figure of speech.

Naturally King devoted the majority of his words to this deliberative part of his speech (to use the term for the branch of rhetoric devoted to persuading someone to do something) – 1,056 out of a total of 1,756, to be pedantic. Then, so the story goes, Mahalia Jackson, standing with the crowd of King's supporters on the podium, shouted over the general din, 'Tell them about the Dream, Martin!' And that's when he laid aside his script and launched into his now-legendary 'I have a dream' peroration.

It may be true. In his book on the speech Gary Younge quotes historian Charles Euchner to the effect that a guest in his hotel had overheard King rehearsing the 'Dream' segment the night before, and that there was too much noise and commotion on the podium for King to have heard Jackson anyway.[8] What does seem to be certain, though, is that Clarence Jones, another King advisor who had had a hand in drafting the official speech, was heard to say at that point, 'These people don't know it, but they're about to go to church.'

What he meant, of course, was that King, for so long the pastor of the Dexter Avenue Baptist Church in Montgomery, Alabama, was about to launch one of those great call-and-response sermons that so characterize the black Baptist, Methodist and Pentecostal churches, in which the preacher's (often improvised) words are as much intoned as spoken, and are punctuated by the congregation's shouts of 'Yes, sir!' and 'Yes, Lord!' and 'Praise God!' and 'All right!' and 'Thank you, Jesus!' Like jazz, the black sermon is one of the great American cultural productions.

'Although King permitted his sermons to be published', Dolan Hubbard explains, 'he knew that the
dynamic interplay between the preacher and the
congregation has much to do with the composition of
the sermon.'[9] That word 'interplay' is well chosen. In the
online recordings one can make out the occasional verbal
responses amid the general applause. But typically the
call-and-response traffic is not all one way. Lyndrey A.
Niles points out that as well as offering feedback, the
congregation often prompts the preacher 'to new heights
of oratorical excellence and insightful sermonizing'.[10] So
Mahalia Jackson's 'tell them about the Dream, Martin'
was right in the tradition of the African American
sermon. Above all, the two-way flow underscores just
how integrated speaker and audience were that day.

And certainly Jackson's intervention did move – or
release – 'new heights of oratorical excellence'. The 700
words beginning with 'I say to you, my friends, so even
though we face the difficulties of today and tomorrow,
I still have a dream' are what people remember today,
often to the exclusion of the main body of the speech.
Once again the insistent anaphora of 'I have a dream'
is enlivened by pauses, run-ons and variations in stress.
Moreover, the paragraphs introduced by the phrase are
not merely repetitive; they form a sequence. The first
goes back to foundations, recapitulating the Declaration:
'I have a dream that one day this nation will rise out and
live out the true meaning of its creed: "We hold these
truths to be self-evident, that all men are created equal."'

The second, third and fifth specify regions, 'the red
hills of Georgia . . . the state of Mississippi . . . down in

Alabama', still in most urgent need of the dream. Finally, after a single reprise of the phrase, 'I have a dream today', he ends in the ecstatic future, now using one of the most powerful prophesies in the Bible – on which Handel also drew for *The Messiah* – Isaiah 40:4:

> I have a dream that one day every valley shall be exalted, every hill and mountain shall be laid low, the rough places will be made plain, and the crooked places will be made straight, and the glory of the Lord shall be revealed, and all flesh shall see it together.

But, of course, the Bible lies behind this speech generally, not just the 'dream' section. Consider this passage:

> No, no, we are not satisfied, and we will not be satisfied until justice rolls down like waters and righteousness like a mighty stream . . . Some of you have come from areas where your quest for freedom left you battered by the storms of persecution and staggered by the winds of police brutality.

What makes this sound so biblical? There are two strongly characteristic features in this word placement. The first is the parallelism of 'waters . . . stream' and 'battered . . . brutality', an echo of the special kind of distich, or pair of verse lines, so fundamental to Hebrew poetry. These are not couplets, much less rhyming couplets, but parallel statements, either synonymous, as in 'Pride goes before destruction, / And a haughty spirit before a fall' (Proverbs 16:18), or antithetical, as in 'The merciful man does good to his own soul, / But he that is cruel troubles his own flesh' (Proverbs 11:17). The other biblical echo is a characteristic figure that is hard to describe (and so far as I know has no name in the list of classical rhetorical terms), except to say that it links a commonplace (usually, though not inevitably a concrete one) – something we all know and experience, like a household utensil or a season of the year or phase of the weather – with an abstraction. The figure has seeped into British poetry, as in Shakespeare's *Richard III*'s 'Now is the winter of our discontent', or Robert Burns's 'We'll tak' a cup o' kindness' in 'Auld Lang Syne', or 'Nights of insult' in W. H. Auden's 'Lay Your Sleeping Head'.

In the Bible it is especially common in the prophetic books, as, for example, in Jeremiah 16:7, 'Neither shall man give them the cup of consolation', and Isaiah 45:8, 'You heavens above, rain down my righteousness; let the clouds shower it down' – both a distich and a common abstract conjunction, and clearly a source for King's 'until justice rolls down like water'. Other powerful uses of this figure are King's 'the whirlwinds of revolt', 'let us not wallow in the valley of despair', 'the table of brotherhood' and 'an oasis of freedom and brotherhood'.

And the trope occurs most densely in that magisterial paragraph defending his discipleship of Mahatma Gandhi's non-violent protest, with an implied warning against those like Malcolm X and the black Nation of Islam, who argued for more direct action:

But there is something that I must say to my people who stand on the warm threshold which leads into the palace of justice. In the process of gaining our rightful place we must not be guilty of wrongful deeds. Let us not seek to satisfy our thirst for freedom by drinking from the cup of bitterness and hatred. We must forever conduct our struggle on the high plane of dignity and discipline. We must not allow our creative protest to degenerate into physical violence. Again and again we must rise to the majestic heights of meeting physical force with soul force.

The power of this speech to persuade depends on its clear argument, but its potential to move the people to a spirit of unity derives from its reference to a shared culture, a common readership. But what reading (or hearing or watching) do Americans – black and white, from all classes and regions of the country – have in common? Not Shakespeare, not Melville, nor even Mark Twain. But the Bible, yes – at least in King's audience in 1963, many of whom had brought their Bibles with them.

And for those without Bibles, there are always popular songs. Many people have forgotten that directly following his magnificent 'I have a dream' passage is a lengthy quotation of 'My Country 'tis of Thee'. Like 'Hail, Columbia!' this was long a sort of unofficial national anthem, before 'The Star-spangled Banner' was formally adopted as such, as late as 1931. Set to the tune of 'God Save the King', though celebrating a very different political outlook, it has remained a popular favourite. Everyone knows it.

He is, after all, appealing for *peaceful* resistance and *inclusive* rights – for all colours and classes of Americans.

Finally, this speech is far more than an appeal for black civil rights. King realized that black progress would also liberate whites – from suspicion, rancour, fear, guilt, revenge – and that's why the speech culminates in the repeated refrain from the song, 'Let freedom ring!' – not just from the regions of troubled race relations, like the 'Stone Mountains of Georgia' and the 'Lookout Mountains of Tennessee' but also from 'the prodigious hilltops of New Hampshire', the 'snow-capped Rockies of Colorado' and the 'curvaceous slopes of California'. The vast spread of geography, so excitingly evoked, involves all regions and all sorts of American.

PART THREE

The Movies: The Rise and Fall
of the Moral Moment

The Great American Speech pops up in all kinds of films, including political thrillers and action movies. Sometimes at length, sometimes in only a few lines of dialogue, the speech widens the moral perspective, always serving to offer a vision of hope, or at least conventional morality, in contrast to the squabbling, competitive, sometimes violent everyday world of the film's setting and action.

In *Casablanca* (dir. Michael Curtiz, 1942), one of the most popular and successful films of all time, the explicit moral lesson is very brief. It comes when Rick Blaine (Humphrey Bogart) tells Ilsa Lund (Ingrid Bergman) that she must go and escape with her husband, Victor Lazlo (Paul Henreid), rather than stay behind in Casablanca with him. This comes as a surprise, not only to her, but to the movie's audience, because we had thought that the two had rediscovered and reaffirmed their love and were never to be separated again as they had been after the Germans invaded Paris. Indeed, such was the lack of plot logic leading to this ending that the actors were told to hold open the possibility that love would conquer virtue after all.

Not only that, but although Rick is capable of personal acts of kindness, as when he arranges for the Bulgarian refugee Jan to win big at roulette so that his young wife can buy their exit visas from Captain Renault instead of having to prostitute herself to him, he has posed up to now as being bitterly detached from expressions of emotion and cynical about the war's aims. 'I stick my neck out for nobody', he tells the (really) cynical Renault (Claude Raines), who responds, 'A wise foreign policy.' To Laszlo Rick poses the question: 'Don't you sometimes wonder if it's worth all this? I mean what you're fighting for?'

But no, when he finally comes to reflect seriously on the public and private imperatives of the world situation – the Second World War, Lazlo's important work as a leader of the resistance and his need for his wife's help in that project – Rick has a sudden pang of conscience, expressed rather patronizingly as something she, the emotional woman, has yet to grasp:

Ilsa: But what about us?
Rick: We'll always have Paris. We didn't have, we, we lost it until you came to Casablanca. We got it back last night.
Ilsa: When I said I would never leave you.
Rick: And you never will. But I've got a job to do, too. Where I'm going, you can't follow. What I've got to do, you can't be any part of. Ilsa, I'm no good at being noble, but it doesn't take much to see that the problems of three little people don't amount to a hill of beans in this crazy world. Someday you'll understand that.
[Ilsa lowers her head and begins to cry]

As for Rick, he and Renault walk off into the mist pledg-ing 'the beginning of a beautiful friendship'. Clearly they were heading off to do important war work. A later scene was planned to show them on a ship preparing to take part in the Allied landing in North Africa, but Rains wasn't available to shoot it.

Maybe Rick was following the lead of Rhett Butler (Clark Gable) in *Gone With the Wind* (dir. Victor Fleming, 1939), who presents himself as a cynical, sexually pro-miscuous gun-runner with no interest in 'the cause' of the Confederacy. 'I believe in the cause of Rhett Butler', he tells a disbelieving Scarlett O'Hara (Vivien Leigh), 'he's the only cause I know.' Yet when she is trapped in Atlanta, Rhett emerges from a brothel to steal a horse and cart to carry Scarlett, Melanie (Olivia de Havilland), her baby and their personal slave Prissy (Butterfly McQueen) free of the burning city, then sets them down on road to Tara.

She's on her own now, he tells her, and can find her own way home. He's off at last to join the Confederate Army. Scarlett, as usual taking even the noblest of Rhett's gestures as a personal affront, demands: 'Rhett, how could you do this to me, and why should you go now that, after it's all over and I need you, why? Why?' He answers: 'Why? Maybe it's because I've always had a weakness for lost causes, once they're really lost. Or maybe, maybe I'm ashamed of myself. Who knows?'

A similar (and much later) jolt into moral awareness – although this time out of comic melodrama rather than historical romance – occurs in Joel and Ethan Coen's masterpiece, *Fargo* (1996). Sheriff Marge Gunderson

(Frances McDormand), seemingly eleven months pregnant, has doggedly tracked the kidnappers of Jean Lundegaard (Kristin Rudrüd) to a cabin on a frozen lake. Between them, the inept Carl Showalter and the sinister Gaear Grimsrud (Steve Buscemi and Peter Storemare) have already killed four people: a highway patrolman, an innocent couple who they think may have witnessed that shooting, and Jean's father, who recklessly pulled a gun on Carl when handing over the ransom money. Now Jean Lundegaard is dead, because, as Gaear puts it, 'she started shrieking, y'know. She wouldn't stop.'

The two men quarrel over how to split the ransom. Gaear hits Carl over the head with an axe, and when Marge come across him, is busy stuffing bits of his body into a wood-chipper that spews red matter over the white snow. Marge challenges Gaear; he runs out over the lake; she brings him down with a shot to his left leg. Cut to a scene in Marge's prowl car, with Gaear in the back:

> Marge Gunderson: So that was Mrs Lundegaard on the floor in there. And I guess that was your accomplice in the wood-chipper. And those three people in Brainerd. And for what? For a little bit of money. There's more to life than a little money, you know. Don'tcha know that? And here ya are, and it's a beautiful day. Well. I just don't understand it.

Marge has the only moral perspective in the film. All the others are crazed by greed or the lust for power, or both, motives never entirely offset by the comic ineptitude with which they try to carry them out. Their victims, including the hapless Jean Lundegaard, seem barely to register as characters, let alone moral beings.

Marge alone is happily married and good at her job. She is about to bring a new life into the world, and can appreciate a beautiful day, even in midwinter. Both her innocence and her professionalism are underlined through-out by her use of childish slang phrases like 'You betcha!' and stock police terminology – sometimes comic in the cir-cumstances – like her explanation to Jerry Lundegaard (William H. Macy) that she's 'investigating some mal-feasance' and later, when he sneaks out of the office and drives away in one of his firm's used cars, 'Oh, for Pete's sake, he's fleeing the interview! He's fleeing the interview!'

Sometimes the speech widens the perspective in respect of class, suddenly prompting the audience's imagination to consider what ordinary people feel and think. *It's a Wonderful Life* (dir. Frank Capra, 1946) has become a classic feelgood film, always replayed on TV over the Christmas holidays, yet when it first came out, the Los Angeles field office of the FBI thought it was highly sub-versive, slating it for its communist sympathies, because it cast a banker as the bad guy.[1]

The framing narrative concerns a despondent George Bailey (James Stewart) about to commit suicide on Christmas Eve because his uncle has lost a crucial $8,000 he needs to deposit in the bank to keep his building and loan company from going bankrupt, and Mr Potter, the bank president, played by Lionel Barrymore, is about to swear out a warrant against him for bank fraud.

Moved by widespread prayers from George's numerous family and friends, Heaven dispatches an apprentice angel called Clarence (Henry Travers) to intervene in his despair. Clarence reminds George of his many good deeds that helped other people and, indeed, the community at large. When he was only twelve George saved his younger brother from drowning, who then went on to save hundreds of others when as a Second World War navy pilot he shot down an enemy plane about to bomb a troop ship.

Later, while working in a drugstore, George prevented the pharmacist from mistakenly filling a child's prescription with poison. Then he gave up his ambition to travel and go to college in order to stay behind in Bedford Falls, to manage, and then salvage, his father's building and loan company.

At one point, when a run on the bank threatens the business, he uses the $2,000 set aside for his honeymoon to plug the gap. As part of his project to provide credit for the working poor he sets up Bailey Park, an affordable housing project. Though his ambitions to travel and study and see the world have all been thwarted, he is widely admired, even loved, and is himself a loving husband and father of four.

To counteract his pessimistic review of his existence, Clarence offers George a vision of what life would be like had he never lived. Bedford Falls would be called Potterville, because Potter's bank would own all of it. Prostitution, gambling and nightclubs would be rife downtown. Bailey Park would not have been built, the pharmacist would be in jail and the American troops at the bottom of the ocean. Of course, George decides to live.

Within the framing narrative the plot plays out the perennial struggle between Potter's bank and the Bailey family building and loan company. It's a class conflict: Potter's business caters to those who have already accumulated capital, or inherited it; Bailey's offers reasonable mortgages which working families can repay from the security of their own homes. At one point Potter comes close to convincing the board managing the building and loan company to close it down, on the grounds that the business is dead in the water after the death of George's father:

Henry F. Potter: Now, you take this loan here to Ernie Bishop – you know, that fellow that sits around all day on his brains in his taxi . . . I happen to know the bank turned down this loan, but he comes here and we're building him a house worth five thousand dollars. Why? . . . You see, if you shoot pool with some employee here, you can come and borrow money. What does that get us? A discontented, lazy rabble instead of a thrifty working class. And all because a few starry-eyed dreamers like Peter Bailey stir them up and fill their heads with a lot of impossible ideas. Now, I say –

George Bailey: Just a minute. Just a, just a minute. Now, hold on, Mr Potter . . . You . . . you said . . . uh – what'd you say just a minute ago? They, they had to wait and save their money before they even thought of a decent home. Wait! Wait for what? Until their children grow up and leave them? Until they're so old and broken-down [cut to Mr Potter stifling a yawn] that they – Do you know how long it takes a working man to save five thousand dollars?

Just remember this, Mr Potter, that this rabble you're talking about – they do most of the working and paying and living and dying in this community. Well, is it too much to have them work and pay and live and die in a couple of decent rooms and a bath?

George wins the board over; they vote to keep the business going, so long as he stays behind in Bedford Falls to run it, instead of going off to college.

Platoon (dir. Oliver Stone, 1986) is no place for speeches, grounded as it is in the realistic portrayal of an infantry platoon under fire in the Vietnam War, but Chris Taylor (Charlie Sheen) gets something of that reflective commentary to be found in movie speeches through the letters he writes to his grandmother, which the audience hear as a voiceover:

Well, here I am, anonymous, all right. With guys nobody really cares about. They come from the end of the line, most of them, small towns you never heard of: Pulaski, Tennessee; Brandon, Mississippi; Pork Bend, Utah; Wampum, Pennsylvania. Two years' high school's about it. Maybe if they're lucky, a job waiting for them back in a factory. But most of 'em got nothing. They're poor. They're the unwanted. Yet they're fighting for our society and our freedom. It's weird, isn't it? They're the bottom of the barrel, and they know it. Maybe that's why they call themselves grunts, 'cause a grunt can take it, can take anything. They're the best I've ever seen, Grandma. The heart and soul.

'The heart and soul' – of what, though? Their unit? The war in Vietnam? The unfinished sentence could also be completed as 'of our country'. Like George Bailey's working families, the grunts in *Platoon* do most of the living – and especially dying – in and for this community. And this community is also the country.

This theme of the working class signing up to fight for the society that all but ignores them is taken up by a later war think-piece. In *Lions for Lambs* (dir. Robert Redford, 2007) three plots unravel in real time. In Washington an ambitious senator played by Tom Cruise calls in a tame TV reporter (Meryl Streep) to offer her the exclusive on a new strategy to take the high ground in Afghanistan, while in Los Angeles a professor of political science has called in for a consultation an apathetic student performing below his potential, and the new strategy is already going wrong in a bungled air assault that lands the American troops in the wrong place.

By contrast to *Platoon*, this prolix screenplay offers plenty of scope for speeches. Here is the professor (Robert Redford) talking about two of his least apathetic and most promising students, a Mexican American and an African American, whom he had tried to persuade not to enlist:

Professor Malley: They went to these high schools where … [there were] metal detectors on every door, teachers carrying Mace. These awful places did them not one favour. I saw the same thing when I was in Vietnam.

Todd Hayes: What?

Malley: The first guys to sign up to fight are the ones this country really doesn't treat that well. Here are Ernest and Arian growing up in these neighbourhoods where people butcher each other for simple-minded shit. 'You were raised in a neighbourhood two blocks south from mine.' Bam! 'The rims on your car are better than mine.' Bam! What do they do after they scrape themselves up and getting outta there in one piece? They go out to fight for the very country that that all but ignores these neighborhoods.

Meanwhile Ernest and Arian are being blown to bits on a mountain top in Afghanistan.

It's not just the working class that they stand for, of course, but minorities. Other groups of Americans who have been overlooked or under provided for include gays – especially gays with AIDS. In *Philadelphia* (dir. Jonathan Demme, 1993) Tom Hanks played a lawyer with AIDS suing his firm for wrongful dismissal. Twenty years before, in real life, Harvey Milk had become the first openly gay politician to be elected to significant public office in California when he won a seat on San Francisco's Board of Supervisors, who, along with the mayor, run the city.

But Milk wasn't just gay; he campaigned actively for gay rights. As he and his cause grew in political credibility, he began to attract death threats. Just a year after his election Milk was indeed assassinated, along with

Mayor George Moscone, by another supervisor, an ex-cop with a grudge, strongly against gay rights being written into law, and an equally strong supporter of a state-wide law to prevent gays from teaching in the California public schools.

For *Milk* (dir. Gus Van Sant, 2008) Sean Penn won an Oscar for his portrayal of the slain supervisor. The movie opens and closes with a recording Milk made 'to be played only in the event of my death by assassination'. So the film's last lines are Milk's voiceover, as spoken by Penn:

I ask this . . . If there should be an assassination, I would hope that five, ten, one hundred, a thousand would rise. I would like to see every gay lawyer, every gay architect come out – If a bullet should enter my brain, let that bullet destroy every closet door . . . And that's all. I ask for the movement to continue. Because it's not about personal gain, not about ego, not about power . . . it's about the 'us's' out there. Not only gays, but the Blacks, the Asians, the disabled, the seniors, the us's. Without hope, the us's give up – I know you cannot live on hope alone, but without it, life is not worth living. So you, and you, and you . . . You gotta give 'em hope . . . you gotta give 'em hope.

Now the arc of the forgotten is widened to embrace other minorities beyond Milk's constituency. As in *Platoon*, the reference opens out to invite all the 'us's'. Taken together, the minorities become the majority.

In other words, in widening sympathy for an overlooked and underprivileged class, the Great American

Speech often opens the appeal to and for the American people as a whole. This is what happens at the end of John Ford's truly great film *The Grapes of Wrath* (1940). And to produce that ending Ford had to depart from the book radically.

John Steinbeck's *The Grapes of Wrath* (1939) traces the break-up of the Joad family as they leave their drought-struck farm in Oklahoma and head west to look for work on the massive one-crop ranches of California. First Granpa dies, then Granma. Then Noah the preacher and Connie, the husband of their daughter Rose of Sharon, defect. Their son Tom goes into hiding. Finally, they are cut off even from the next generation as Rose of Sharon's baby is stillborn.

There was a conflict in Steinbeck between, on the one hand, his superb powers of observation, his sympathy for the Okies and his skill in dramatizing their predicament, and, on the other, his saturation in the old literary tradition of Frank Norris and other California naturalists, in which a story, to be true, always had to end with the power of raw nature swallowing up human endeavour, however worthy.

Steinbeck the imaginative journalist could document not only the terrible conditions of the Okies' work and life in California, but also the way the government was helping with measures like their so-called 'sanitary' camps for farm migrants, offering cabins or tents on platforms, bathrooms and showers, community activities, child care, basic medical care and immunity from farm-owner vigilantes coming in to break union organization.

That other Steinbeck, the self-consciously literary novelist, had to have a tragedy and a sacrifice. Hence the grisly and unlikely ending of *The Grapes of Wrath*, which Steinbeck had planned from the beginning, in which the Joads are backed up by a flood against the wall of a barn with nowhere to go, and Rose of Sharon offers the milk intended for her baby to the lips of an old man starving to death.[2]

When he came to make the film John Ford was having none of this. His movie shares the style, and the more hopeful tone of those New Deal documentaries, like *The River* (dir. Pare Lorentz, 1938) and *The Power and the Land* (dir. Joris Ivens, 1940), in which human agency can overcome the ravages of flood and drought. Ford frees the Joads from their apocalyptic stasis and puts them back on the road, on their way north from a government camp for migrant farm workers to the promise of twenty days' cotton picking near Fresno.

The scene is shot as though looking in through the car windscreen:

Pa: We sure taken a beatin'.
Ma: I know. That's what makes us tough. Rich fellas come up an' they die, an' their kids ain't no good an' they die out. But we keep acomin'. We're the people that live. They can't wipe us out; they can't lick us. We'll go on forever, Pa, 'cause we're the people.

These are the last words in the film. The germ of this speech appears in the book, two chapters before the ending, following Ma's famous distinction between men and women: 'Man, he lives in jerks ... Women, it's all one flow, like a stream'. She goes on to say, 'People is goin' on – changing a little, maybe, but goin' right on.'

Nunally Johnson, who wrote the screenplay, added Ma's 'Rich fellas', reinforcing the class conflict, but then – by inserting that crucial definite article to Ma's more general 'people' – turns the 'we' who aren't rich or fortunate into 'the people' – that is the American *demos*, not just poor but rich and middling too. So the last three words of the film echo the first three of the American Constitution: 'We the people . . .'.

By the mid-1980s the Great American Speech was well enough known to act as an ironic counterweight to the words as spoken on screen. Gordon Gekko's 'Greed is good' speech in *Wall Street* (dir. Oliver Stone, 1987) creates a sense of shock not just because it unsettles the audience within the film – after all, as shareholders of the Teldar Paper Company they might be expected to react to the man trying to take them over – but also because it confronts and inverts the Great American Speech so brusquely and explicitly:

Gordon Gekko [Michael Douglas]: The new law of evolution in corporate America seems to be survival of the unfittest. Well, in my book you either do it right or you get eliminated. In the last seven deals that I've been involved with, there were 2.5 million stockholders who have made a pretax profit of 12 billion dollars. [APPLAUSE] Thank you. I am not a destroyer of companies. I am a liberator of them! The point is, ladies and gentleman, that greed, for lack of a better word, is good. Greed is right, greed works. Greed clarifies, cuts through, and captures the essence of the evolutionary spirit. Greed, in all of its forms;

greed for life, for money, for love, knowledge has marked the upward surge of mankind. And greed, you mark my words, will not only save Teldar Paper, but that other malfunctioning corporation called the USA. Thank you very much.

Real-life Wall Street traders loved Gekko's chutzpah and imitated his red braces, but the movie makes him into one of those old serio-comic villains out of a medieval morality play. It starts with his symbolic name, suggesting a wily Southeast Asian reptile, and it ends with his richly deserved indictment and imprisonment. The movie's audience has already heard him brief his ambitious disciple, Bud Fox (Charlie Sheen): 'Now you're not naive enough to think we're living in a democracy, are you buddy? It's the free market. And you're a part of it.'

This comes over as one of those asides in Shakespeare's *Richard III* (another morality-play derivative), in which the eponymous villain says things like 'Conscience is but a word that cowards use, / Devised at first to keep the strong in awe.'

So when we join that other audience in the Teldar Paper stockholders' meeting, we are fully prepared for Gekko's bravura demolition, almost point by point, of such pieties as are proclaimed in *It's a Wonderful Life*. But the message comes over as surprising, perhaps even amusingly daring, because of the lingering normative power of the Great American Speech. In other words, far from undermining the values of the Great American Speech, *Wall Street* reinforces them, because it depends on them for its comic-shock impact.

But by the time we reach 2012 and *Killing Them Softly* (dir. Andrew Dominik), the challenge to those ideals feels very different. Hit man Jackie Cogan (Brad Pitt) joins his controller (Richard Jenkins) in a bar, expecting to be paid for two murders he has just carried out to order. They argue over the amount owed. On the wall-mounted TV Barack Obama is delivering something very closely resembling the Great American Speech.

> Barack Obama: . . . to reclaim the American dream and reaffirm that fundamental truth, that, out of many, we are one . . .
>
> Driver: You hear that line? Line's for you.
>
> Cogan: Don't make me laugh. One people. It's a myth created by Thomas Jefferson.
>
> Driver: Oh, so now you're going to have a go at Jefferson, huh?
>
> Cogan: My friend, Thomas Jefferson is an American saint because he wrote the words 'All men are created equal', words he clearly didn't believe since he allowed his own children to live in slavery. He's a rich white snob who's sick of paying taxes to the Brits. So, yeah, he writes some lovely words and aroused the rabble and they went and died for those words while he sat back and drank his wine and fucked his slave girl. This guy wants to tell me we're living in a community? Don't make me laugh. I'm living in America, and in America you're on your own. America's not a country. It's just a business. Now fuckin' pay me.

Unlike Gordon Gekko's 'Greed is Good' speech, this is not a daring challenge; it is a deconstruction. That is, it draws attention not only to the text of the Declaration of Independence, but also to the economic, political and social conditions of its production. After Cogan has done with it, the Declaration can stand no longer purely as disembodied words conveying a universal meaning. The cynicism of Cogan's hit may have marked the end of the Great American Speech in the movies. That's quite a hit.

7

Six Monuments and a Filibuster:
The Other Discourse of *Mr Smith*
Goes to Washington

There are a lot of fancy words here. Some of them are
carved in stone by men so suckers like me could read
them. Then you find out what those men actually do.
I'm getting out of this town so fast. Away from all the
words, the monuments, the whole rotten show.

THIS IS JAMES STEWART's character speaking in
Mr Smith Goes to Washington: Jefferson Smith, whose
name proclaims both his ordinariness and his affiliation
to the Founding Fathers. At this late point in Frank
Capra's masterpiece, Smith is not going to Washington
but is about to leave it because his idealistic project
for a boys' summer camp has just been thwarted by an
unscrupulous gang of financial manipulators who plan
to build a dam on the land Smith had intended for
his camp.

After an initial flurry of controversy stirred up by the
Washington press and real-life senators who thought that
the production reflected badly on the American system
of government, the movie did well at the box office and
was nominated for eleven Oscars. It has since become a
classic, lodged by the Library of Congress in the National

Film Registry as 'culturally, historically and aesthetically significant'.

Smith's late scorn for monuments comes as a shock, since for most of the film he has been in awe of them. Indeed his response to monuments and the speeches they embody serve as pivotal points in the film's action. Newly arrived in the city as an appointee to fill out the term of a senator who has died in office, the naive and idealistic leader of the Boy Rangers gives his reception party the slip to take a tour bus round the monuments. The tour is presented as a montage involving the Capitol Building, the Washington Monument, the Jefferson Memorial (with a close-up of the Declaration) and Arlington Cemetery.

At the Lincoln Memorial, where Smith gets out of the bus, the montage gives way to real-time action. For the first of three occasions in the film, Smith walks up the stairs towards the imposing statue of the seated president. He gazes at the speeches on the walls. A little boy, coached by his father, reads out the Gettysburg Address haltingly, while an African American, old enough to have been one of the slaves freed by the Emancipation Proclamation, enters the hall in silent reverence. The soundtrack glosses the action with first, for the nation, the 'Star-spangled Banner', and then the 'Battle Hymn of the Republic', for the Union cause.

Smith finally reaches his office, five hours late. It is night, but Saunders, his hard-boiled secretary (Jean Arthur), is still waiting for him.

> Smith: I'm awfully sorry. It wasn't until I was fairly well along on the bus . . .

Saunders: Did you say *bus*?

Smith: It was one of those sightseers ... I've never been called absent-minded before. But there it was all of a sudden, staring right at me at the station.

Saunders: There what was?

Smith: The dome. The Capitol dome. Big as life. Sparkling away under the old sun. I just started to go towards it, and there was a bus outside. And I just naturally got aboard.

Saunders: Most natural thing in the world.

Smith: I don't think I've ever been so thrilled in my life.

That Capitol dome will recur thrice. Meanwhile, there is the wonder of the Lincoln Memorial to relate:

Smith: And that Lincoln Memorial ... Gee whiz! Mr Lincoln, there he is. He's just looking straight at you as you come up those steps. Just ... sitting there like he was waiting for somebody to come along.

Saunders [thinking of how long she has been waiting for him, but probably also of her marital status]: Yeah, Well, he's got nothing on me.

Later in a taxi Smith keeps pointing to statues and other monuments, asking who or what they represent. Saunders says, 'I wouldn't know in the daytime.' Once again the Capitol dome excites his enthusiasm: 'Look, Look! the Capitol Building's all lighted up! Look at it!' to which Saunders replies with a weary 'You'd better relax, Senator. You'll get yourself plumb wore out', and Smith finally subsides with a final 'Gee whiz.' When Saunders tells him the Senate convenes at 12 noon the next day, he says he will go down to Mount Vernon in the morning, 16 miles south of Washington, to 'visit Washington's home before walking into the Senate for the first time. Don't you think that would be a good idea?' 'Wonderful', replies Saunders in her characteristic deadpan.

What Smith has intuited is that those monuments send Americans back to their founding principles, and hence to their better nature as Americans. In movies like *A Few Good Men* (dir. Rob Reiner, 1992) they appear minimally, but meaningfully. The movie's action, the court martial of two marines accused of murdering a fellow soldier, is punctuated by cutaway shots of the Lincoln and Jefferson memorials, the Washington Monument itself and the U.S. Marine Corps War Memorial (a statue of the Marines raising the flag on Iwo Jima). These shots, taken at night and dramatically lit, just like Smith's Capitol dome, serve not just to fix the trial's location in Washington, but also act as silent statements of what constitutes true valour and justice.

Monuments go much further than that, though, in *Mr Smith Goes to Washington*. Here they make up a continuous strand of reference to those founding values that the corrupt politicians are so carelessly destroying. For the real operators, the men behind the scenes, Smith's 'gee whiz' naivety is laughable, but also useful, because it means they can put all sorts of chicanery over on him. In fact, it's why they got him appointed by the malleable state governor in the first place. The amiable scoutmaster is perfect for the purposes of Jim Taylor (Edward

Arnold), whose bribes and threats control the state political machine, not to mention the press and – most troublesome of all, to Smith – the state's senior senator, Joe Paine.

Paine is the really interesting cog in the Taylor machine. It's a complex role, carefully executed by Claude Rains. Paine is being groomed by Taylor for the White House. He and Smith's father were best friends. 'Dad used to tell me Joe Paine was the finest man he ever knew', as Jeff Smith puts it. On the train to Washington Smith reminds Paine of the old days, when his father, editor of a local newspaper, defended a small miner who didn't want to sell his claim to a large mining syndicate. The syndicate first tried bribing the editor, then threatening him. Finally they had him shot in the back.

> Paine: Clayton Smith, editor and publisher. Champion of lost causes.
> Smith: Dad always said those were the only worthy causes.
> Paine: You don't have to tell me. We were a team. The struggling editor and the struggling lawyer.

Smith's initial enthusiasm for Washington soon gives way to humiliation. Newspaper coverage presents him as a naive country bumpkin. When he goes to the Press Club looking for reporters to take a swing at, he soon discovers the source of their scorn. They accuse him of being a 'Christmas tiger',[1] who 'will nod his head and vote ... just like his colleague tells him to', and 'an honorary stooge' to do the bidding of the Taylor machine.

Hurt and puzzled, Smith seeks out Paine for an explanation. Paine doesn't answer directly, but deflects Smith's queries by suggesting he use his time in the Senate to introduce a bill:

Paine: Didn't you say something to the papers about wanting to create a boys' camp? Now, you were in earnest about that, weren't you?

Smith: Yes.

Paine: Why don't you do it? Get a bill started. Present it to Congress. It'll be great experience for you.

Smith: I've been aching to mention it to you. If I could just do that one thing, I'd feel . . .

Paine: What's to stop you? Saunders'll help.

Smith: I will do it. I knew that if anyone could help me, you could.

Fired up now and forgetting his humiliation, Smith goes back to his office to ask Saunders's help. 'Senator', she replies in exasperation, 'have you any idea what it takes to get a bill passed?' When she has gone through some of the steps – first reading, committee stage, reference to the House of Representatives, the vote there, reference to the steering committee of majority leaders, return to the Senate – he interrupts, pointing through the window:

Smith: That's what has got to be in it.

Saunders: What?

Smith: The Capitol dome.

Saunders: On paper?

Smith: It should come to life for every boy. All lighted

up too. Boys forget what their country means by just reading 'Land of the Free' in history books. Men forget even more. Liberty is too precious a thing to be buried in books. Men should hold it up in front of them every single day and say: 'I'm free . . . to think and to speak. My ancestors couldn't. I can. And my children will.' . . . Boys ought to remember that.

Smith wants to build the camp in Terry Canyon, on Willet Creek, which he feelingly evokes in the one extended descriptive passage in the whole screenplay:

Smith: You've never been there, Miss Saunders? I've been over every single foot. You have to see it for yourself. The prairies, wind leaning on the grass. Lazy streams, . . . water up in the mountains, cattle moving down the slope against the sun, campfires and snowdrifts . . .

So the next day Smith rises to present his bill on the Senate floor. His voice quaking with nerves, his notes shaking in his hand, he proposes a federal loan to be raised for the boys' camp, the Treasury to be repaid by contributions from boys all over America. Up in the visitors' gallery boys cheer. Already by the next day contributions begin to come in. Smith arrives at the Senate Office building, whistling as he strides down the corridor. Suddenly he's a celebrity. Outside his office people try to catch his attention, wanting to handle his publicity account, asking favours, trying to interest him in investments.

He feels great. 'Boy, I feel like a house on fire', he tells Saunders. 'Even went down to see Mr Lincoln again. Saunders, how did I do? My heart was right up to here. What do you think Paine thought?' 'He must have been tickled pink', says Saunders laconically. As she well knows, he was anything but. Taylor and his cronies have already bought up Terry Canyon and primed Paine to sponsor a bill to build a dam there.

When they hear of Smith's project, Taylor's pals are horrified. Taylor himself comes to Washington, where one of his henchmen tells him, 'Honest, Jim, I haven't been able to show him a single monument. [Gestures with thumb and forefinger nearly touching.] Not even one that high.' That's how bad things have got: Smith can no longer be diverted by monuments.

As Smith comes up against the Taylor machine it becomes clear that his respect for monuments and the principles they represent, or often actually embody in the form of engraved speeches, is not just an index of his naivety but also a necessary alternative discourse, a way of engaging with American democratic ideals that is wholly distinct from the language of compromise and accommodation that makes government happen in the real world.

That same, perhaps unconscious, motive lies behind his other (philosophical) form of naivety, that the Capitol dome can somehow be transferred bodily to the words on paper that will make up his boys' camp bill. In his confusion, his inexperience in the complexities of political discourse, he wants to reify abstractions, get them tied down once again to those three-dimensional objects that in turn represent another, purer set of abstractions, like equality, opportunity and the freedom to speak and vote.

What he is trying to get away from – again, probably unconsciously – is the kind of language Paine uses when trying to soften Smith's disillusionment on learning that his father's most admired best friend is involved with the Taylor machine:

> Paine: I know how you feel. I was hoping you'd be spared all this. That you'd see the sights, absorb a lot of history and go back to your boys. You've been living in a boy's world. For heaven's sake, stay there! This is a man's world, a brutal world. You have no place in it. You'll only get hurt. Forget Taylor and what he said about the dam.
>
> Smith: And those other men tell you what to do?
>
> Paine: Now – listen, please. And try to understand. I know it's tough to run head-on into facts. But you must check your ideals outside the door like you do your rubbers. Thirty years ago, I had your ideals. I was you. I had to make the same decision you were asked to make today. And I made it. I compromised. Yes. So that all those years I could sit in that Senate and serve the people in an honest way. You've gotta face facts, Jeff. I've served our state well, haven't I? We have the lowest unemployment and the highest federal grants, but – well, I've had to compromise.

In terms of his own discourse Paine is a good workaday politician – perhaps better than that. In the New Deal era high federal grants and low unemployment are signs that he is serving his constituents well. For that matter, you could argue that a new dam, however compromised by graft, would be of far more use than a boys' camp, or at least that a boys' camp might be just as well be located in some other picturesque part of the state.

But Paine's revealing assumption that there is an absolute disconnect between, on the one hand, the business of government and, on the other, seeing the sights and absorbing 'a lot of history' reinforces Smith's case. What, after all, is the point of the Washington monuments? Are they merely tourist attractions, or do they somehow represent the aspirations and achievements of the American political process?

So Smith lives in another discourse. Because of his idealism – or naivety, if that is what it is – he will not compromise, will not accommodate. He gets up in the Senate to block the bill that includes the dam on Willet Creek, insisting on his own prior project. Taylor and his cronies respond breathtakingly by accusing Smith himself of graft, and it is Paine who sticks the knife in:

> Paine: I refer to the bill he has introduced for the creation of a boys' camp. He named a certain portion of land – to be bought by contributions from boys all over America. Senators, I have evidence that he owns the very land described in his bill. He bought it the day following his appointment to the Senate – and is holding it, using his privileged office for his own personal profit!

A hearing follows of the Committee of Privileges. Stooges hired by Taylor testify to Smith having signed contracts and deeds that prove his culpability. 'Experts' testify for and against the authenticity of his signature. Paine recommends expulsion from the Senate. Invited to take the stand, Smith walks out in shock.

It is this defeat that brings him back to the Lincoln Memorial for the third time, to speak the lines with which this chapter opens. Once again Smith has climbed the stairs and gazed, not just at the imposing statue of the seated president, but at the Gettysburg Address on the wall behind it, with the film's lighting picking out the words, 'of the people, by the people, for the people'. It is this sentiment, particularly, that Smith feels has been belied by his experience. In Our Nation's Capitol, he has discovered, the American government does not give a damn about the People.

Now his bitterness is directed as much at the monuments as at the crooks in the Senate, not least because it was the monuments that had promised him so much by way of a clear statement of American ideals. Instead they seem now to exist only to deceive, being the work of wicked men, 'fancy words' carved in stone, expressly to make fools out of 'suckers like me'.

As he turns away from the Gettysburg Address, we see that he actually has his suitcases with him, and is leaving right away. Just then, out of the shadow of a column steps Saunders, whose cynical veneer has been much softened by his predicament. Now she's in the process of falling in love with him. When he tells her he's leaving, she asks:

Saunders: What will you tell the kids back home?

Smith: The truth. They might as well find out now as later.

Saunders: I don't think they'll believe you. They're liable to look at you with hurt faces and say: 'Jeff, what did you do? Quit? Didn't you do something about it?'

Smith: What do you expect me to do? An honorary stooge like me against the Taylors and Paines – the machines and the lies.

Saunders: Your friend Mr Lincoln had his Taylors and Paines. So did every man who ever tried to lift his thought up off the ground. Odds against them didn't stop them, they were fools that way. All the good in this world came from fools with faith like that. You know that Jeff. You can't quit now. Not you. They aren't all Taylors and Paines, that kind just throw big shadows. You didn't just have faith in Paine or any other man. It was bigger than that. You had plain, decent, everyday common rightness. And this country could use some of that. Yeah. So could the whole cock-eyed world. A lot of it. Remember the first day you got here? What you said about Mr Lincoln? You said he was sitting there waiting for someone. You were right. He was waiting for a man who could see his job and sail into it. A man who could tear into the Taylors and root them out into the open. I think he was waiting for you, Jeff. He knows you can do it, so do I.

This is nothing less than the Great American Speech, though expressed informally, in conversation rather than declaimed from a podium – and by a woman at that. Later, Smith will deliver these sentiments in their conventional rhetorical setting, but meanwhile he is intrigued by her suggestion of action:

> Smith: But do what, Saunders?
> Saunders: Say you won't quit and I'll tell you what. I've been thinking about it all day. It's a forty-foot dive into a tub of water, but I think you can do it.

Maybe because her appeal chimes with his father's belief that lost causes are the best causes, and certainly because Saunders's invocation of Lincoln's reinstates his faith in monuments, Smith pauses to think. Finally, for the first time, he uses her first name, hitherto withheld to maintain her hard-boiled image:

> Smith: Clarissa, where can we get a drink?
> Saunders: Now you're talkin'!

The plan she has begun to formulate, though Smith doesn't know it yet and neither does the audience, is that Smith will engage in a monumental filibuster to block the passage of the bill, including the Willet Creek dam. Many people think of filibusters as a twentieth-century American invention, a tactic used by progressives like Kingfish Huey Long to promote his Share Our Wealth programme or southern reactionaries like Strom Thurmond to stonewall against civil rights legislation. In fact, the practice of talking a bill out goes back through the British and Canadian houses of commons to at least as far as Cato the Younger, who would speak against a measure he disliked until nightfall, by which time all business had to be concluded according to a rule of the Roman Senate.

But how to pass the time? What to talk about? Huey Long used to quote Shakespeare at length and read out recipes (of which there are many) for 'pot-likkers' of ham hocks and collard greens. Of course, Smith's own speech, however rambling and seemingly endless, would have to start at the arguments for his boys' camp and a lengthy denunciation of the dam project, but an effective filibuster will have to keep the Senate in session, if necessary for days.

Being Jefferson Smith, he turns to monuments – verbal ones this time – like the Declaration of Independence to confront that other discourse of compromise and accommodation:

> Smith: '. . . with certain unalienable rights. Among these are life, liberty and the pursuit of . . .'
> Reporter [talking into his microphone, and also providing a useful bit of exposition]: The least man in that chamber, once he gets and holds that floor – can talk as long as he can stand on his feet. Providing that he does not sit down, does not leave the chamber or stop talking. The galleries are packed. They have come to see what they can't see at home: democracy in action.
> Smith: '. . . the pursuit of happiness. That, to secure these rights, governments are instituted among men – deriving their just powers from the consent of the

governed; – that whenever any form of government becomes destructive to these ends – it is the right of the people to alter or abolish . . .'

As he gets through the Declaration a page hands him a note from Saunders in the gallery. 'You're wonderful', it reads. 'Press boys all with you. Read them the Constitution next, <u>very slow</u>. Diz [her cynical journalist friend] says I'm in love with you. PS He's right.'

> Smith: The Constitution of the United States. Page one, top left-hand corner: 'We, the people of the United States, in order to form a more perfect union.'

So Smith's filibuster turns out to be monumental in both form and content. While his words are being relayed, through the gallery press corps, back to his home state, Taylor orders the home newspapers, which he controls, to print only the story that Smith, convicted of graft by the Senate Committee on Privileges, is talking endless nonsense simply to block the Senate vote to expel him.

Smith's allies try to get the truth out via the paper his boys produce. Scenes of huge rotary presses rolling out Taylor's lies are intercut with others of frantic boys pulling off single sheets expressing the truth. When the kids take their paper out on the streets, truckloads of hoodlums reminiscent of then-current newsreels of Nazi Germany arrive to beat them over the head and turf their news sheets into the gutter.

Meanwhile Smith has one more monument to cite, the first that caught his eye in Washington. This is when the Great American Speech, first pleaded by Saunders, surfaces in all its rhetorical formality. Here are the usual themes of one among many (regardless of 'race, color or creed'), of corporate civic action supplanting the individualistic law of the jungle:

> Smith: Just get up off the ground. Get up there with that lady on top of the Capitol dome – that lady that stands for liberty. Take a look at this country through her eyes. You won't just see scenery. You'll see what man's carved out for himself. After centuries of fighting for something better than jungle law. Fighting so's he can stand on his own two feet, free and decent, like he was created. No matter what his race, color or creed, that's what you'll see. There's no place out there for graft or greed or lies. Or compromise with human liberties. If that's what the grown-ups have done with this world, we have to start those boys' camps and see what the kids can do. It's not too late. This country is bigger than the Taylors, or you or me or anything else. Great principles don't get lost once they come to light. They're right here. You just have to see them.

There is some confusion here over what it is it that embodies the great principles of American political identity. Is it the seer, the lady representing Freedom, or what she sees 'out there'? Perhaps Smith is just tired. Or maybe, in his final encomium to monuments, he has stumbled upon his most profound perception of their practical civic function: that they not only represent great truths but seem to judge how well we are living up to them.

The great monuments are both seen and seeing. The statue of Freedom is not only seen on top of the Capitol dome but looks out over the social and political landscape – 'you won't just see scenery' – to judge how well we are living up to our collective perspective. Lincoln's gaze – 'looking straight at you as you come up those steps', as Smith puts it – is directed at the individual citizen. It seems to say, how well are you doing? What more can you do to further the causes I fought for?

This is why it is so limiting to think of the Washington monuments as just tourist attractions, famous for being famous, and why Taylor and his cronies are so bent on keeping Smith's presence in the city confined to sightseeing. And though the monuments are useful reminders of the nation's past, they are not confined to that function either, as implied in Paine's wish that Smith could have been content to 'absorb a lot of history'. They are living things, interacting with every citizen in the here and now; not only offering information but asking for it in return.

Smith begins to flag. To hasten his oratorical extinction, Taylor has organized a bogus campaign of constituents' telegrams to the Capitol, urging Smith to yield the floor and stop interrupting the nation's business. They are brought into the chamber. Smith, disbelieving, runs his hands through the mounds of paper, poring over the supposedly hostile sentiments. He is silent a long time. Then at last:

Smith: I guess this is just another lost cause, Mr Paine.
[Turns to the Senate at large.] All you people don't
know about lost causes. Mr Paine does. He said
once they were the only causes worth fighting for.
And he fought for them once, for the only reason
any man ever fights for them. Because of just one
plain, simple rule: Love thy neighbor. In this world
full of hatred a man who knows that one rule has a
great trust. You know that rule, Mr Paine. I loved
you for it, just as my father did. You know that you
fight harder for the lost causes You even die for
them. Like a man we both knew, Mr Paine. You
think I'm licked. You all think I'm licked. Well, I am
not licked! And I'm gonna stay right here and fight
for this lost cause. Even if this room gets filled with
lies like these – And the Taylors and all their armies
come marching into this place. Somebody will listen
to me.

At this point he collapses in exhaustion. But he's only
fainted. Smith's evocation of the Lady Liberty's
perspective, combined with his personal appeal to Paine,
produce a striking denouement. Paine suddenly rushes
from the chamber. Shots are heard. He's tried to kill
himself, but been prevented. Then he runs back in:

Paine: Expel me! Expel me, not him! Willet dam is a
fraud. It's a crime against the people who sent me
here! I committed it! Every word that boy said
about Taylor and me and graft. And the rotten
political corruption of my state is true! I'm not

fit for office! I'm not fit for any place of honor! Expel me!

Smith has won. Saunders is so overjoyed, she drops her wisecracks for childlike glee: 'Hurrah! He did it! Yippee!'

The titles roll to 'Yankee Doodle' and 'My Country 'tis of Thee'.

8

The Great Trial Scene: *The Verdict* and *To Kill a Mockingbird*

JURIES IN AMERICAN courtroom drama represent America itself. That's because 'Courts in this country are the great levelers', as Atticus Finch (Gregory Peck) says in his summing-up speech in *To Kill a Mockingbird* (dir. Robert Mulligan, 1962), the culmination of his defence – unsuccessful, as it turns out – of young black man falsely accused of raping a white woman. 'In our courts, all men are created equal.'

Access to the law is as important to participatory democracy as the right to vote. Furthermore, whatever the case to be decided, jury trials are the model of American society as it was meant to be, hence their popularity in the movies. There, if nowhere else, all men and women really are created equal, just as it says in the Declaration, and the wealthy and powerful can be overthrown in favour of the humble and underprivileged. Or at least, as Andrew Beckett (Tom Hanks) puts it in *Philadelphia*, 'It's that every now and again – not often, but occasionally – you get to be a part of justice being done. That really is quite a thrill when that happens.'

Unfortunately, real-life trials often fall far short of this ideal. There was no thrill of justice, no voice allowed the accused in 1930s Alabama, when nine black teenagers, the youngest of whom were twelve and thirteen, were sentenced to death for allegedly raping two white girls. The trials and re-trials of the so-called Scottsboro Boys lasted an astonishing six years, from 1931 to 1937. They were a national sensation, leading to two successful appeals to the U.S. Supreme Court, not to mention the more general popular outrage generated by coverage in the press outside the South.

What happened was that on 25 March 1931 the nine boys were riding the rails on a freight train when they ran up against four young white men and two women. They got into a fight, and the white boys were forced off the train. Bent on revenge, they reported the fight to the stationmaster at Stevenson, Alabama, who telegraphed ahead to Paint Rock to have the train stopped and the blacks arrested.

At this point the two white women accused the blacks of raping them. The boys were immediately taken to jail in nearby Scottsboro. Later that same day a lynch mob gathered outside the jail, only to be dispersed when the state governor called out the national guard.

The first trial attracted plenty of local interest. According to Hollace Ransdell, a young teacher, journalist and activist who was covering the scene for the American Civil Liberties Union (ACLU), there was almost a carnival atmosphere in Scottsboro. 'People from surrounding counties and states began arriving by car and train with the coming of dawn', she reported. By ten o'clock 'a crowd of 8,000 to 10,000 swarmed in the narrow village streets . . . packing the outside rim of the

Square around the Courthouse with a solid mass of humanity.'[1]

The trial itself was a darker sort of carnival. The defendants were represented by an elderly local lawyer who hadn't tried a case in decades. One of the alleged rape victims was allowed to testify at great length, but was cross-examined ineffectually for only ten minutes. Without enough time to prepare a case, and with no attempt made to call independent witnesses, the defence had to fall back on the boys' own testimony, which was confused and often conflicting. The defence offered no closing statement, so no chance of a Great American Speech there. To no one's surprise the Scottsboro Boys were convicted of rape and sentenced to death.

The verdict was appealed to the u.s. Supreme court which ruled, in *Powell v. Alabama* (1932), that the incompetence of the defence had denied the defendants the citizen's right to due process of law, and that the case would have to be retried. For the new trial the prosecution upped its game, recruiting the Alabama State attorney general to pursue the case. The defence followed suit, by bringing in Samuel Liebowitz, a high-powered New York attorney working *pro bono*. This time the trial paid attention to the girls' medical condition. According to the doctor who had examined them shortly after the alleged incident, they had not been raped at all but had had consensual intercourse at least 24 hours before the fracas on the freight train.

Called as a witness for the defence, one of the girls testified that they were prostitutes, that no rape had taken place and that when they had been picked up in Alabama, the other had told her to 'frame up a story' as a smoke-screen to prevent their own arrest for violating the Mann Act forbidding the crossing of state lines 'for immoral purposes'.

Following the collapse of the prosecution's case, the trial judge had no choice but to set aside the original verdict and sentences. Even so, the State of Alabama clung to its lost cause, pursuing the Scottsboro Boys over another four years of trials and yet another appeal to the Supreme Court, before finally dropping charges against four of the accused. The others would avoid the death penalty and eventually escape or jump parole.

Harper Lee set *To Kill a Mockingbird* in a small Alabama town in the years 1933–5, right in the middle of the long Scottsboro process. But she wrote the better part of it in 1956, the year after another notorious sex–race trial, in which another all-white, all-male jury acquitted the two men who murdered Emmett Till, a young African American from Chicago visiting relatives in Mississippi, for supposedly flirting with a white woman.

By this time the great movement for black civil rights was already under way, sparked off by the landmark Supreme Court decision of *Brown v. Board of Education* (1954), ruling that segregation in public education was unconstitutional. Properly thought through, this judgement invalidated the whole basis of the Jim Crow laws – the legislation enforcing racial segregation – that separate could entail equal.

So Harper Lee set her book in a time when the black community's reaction to injustice might plausibly veer towards passive acceptance of the relative power of the whites – as indeed is the case in both novel and film versions of *To Kill a Mockingbird* – but she wrote and produced it in an atmosphere in which the reaction to any legal injustice to an African American would certainly be incendiary. Following Till's murder his mother had his body brought back to Chicago for his funeral, insisting on an open coffin so that the mourners could see the terrible wounds to her son's head. The outrage was not confined to African Americans. Black news magazines like *Jet* ran the story, but so did mainstream papers across the rest of the country. Politicians became involved. William Faulkner wrote two essays in *Harpers* magazine in 1956. Langston Hughes and Gwendolyn Brooks wrote poems. Bob Dylan wrote and sang 'The Death of Emmett Till'.

When Rosa Parks was arrested for refusing to move back to the 'colored' seats to make way for a white passenger on a bus in Montgomery, Alabama, she started to comply with the driver's order, but then she 'thought of Emmett Till and I just couldn't go back'. The black boycott of the city bus system, which lasted from 1 December 1955 until 20 December 1956, was a landmark, a now legendary act of solidarity in the civil rights campaign.

To Kill a Mockingbird is above all a *Bildungsroman* – that is, a story about growing up. It's not just about the narrator, Scout Finch, but also her brother Jem and their friend Dill Harris, as they confront, and learn to understand, various mysteries to do with the adult world and beliefs: the independent perspective of the spinster Miss Maudie, the isolation of misfits like Boo Radley and Mrs Dubose, issues of class, gender and above all race.

The novel also falls squarely within that embodiment of the tomboy theme in southern fiction – Carson McCullers's *The Member of the Wedding* (1946) is another instance – in which a young girl narrator grows up in the South, receiving wisdom from the African American cook in the kitchen, in the absence of more hands-on parental guidance.

Where the book departs from *The Member of the Wedding,* of course, is in the trial of Tom Robinson, falsely accused of the rape of Mayella Ewell. Tom's trial, which also takes place in a small Alabama town in the 1930s, recalls the original Scottsboro trial. There's the same threat of lynching, deflected this time not by the National Guard but by Atticus himself, sitting on the courthouse steps, and by his daughter talking sweetly to the leader of the mob. There is the same sense of local holiday, with 'no room at the public hitching-rail for another animal, mules and wagons . . . parked under every available tree' and 'picnic parties sitting on newspapers, washing down biscuit and syrup with warm milk from fruit jars'. Like the first of the Scottsboro trials, Tom's trial introduces no medical evidence relating to the victim's condition immediately following the alleged rape.

But why was *To Kill a Mockingbird* set when its author was a girl and not when the book came out? Was it because she wanted to re-cast her narrative stance as that of a precocious but naive child when her father, the model for Atticus Finch, was practising law in the town where she spent her childhood? Or was it a way of looking at the civil rights struggle from an oblique angle, taking the heat out of it by transposing some of the issues it confronted to a less conflicted era? The book's popularity (Pulitzer Prize, five million copies sold by 1964) and the film's equivalent success (three Academy Awards, grossing 6.5 times its budget within a year, not to mention another $7.5 million taken so far in rentals in the U.S. alone) may have something to do with its having offered the public an unthreatening re-staging of contemporary racial tensions – a sort of civil rights-lite.

Was it also to restore justice to the first Scottsboro trial, if only in that wish-fulfilling discourse allowed to fiction? Unlike at the first Scottsboro trial, the defence lawyer in *To Kill a Mockingbird* gets to cross-examine the supposed victim, rigorously enough to reveal that she is lying about the rape. It is also allowed a powerful closing speech.

The film accentuated this stress on justice, making the trial of Tom Robinson relatively more prominent than it is in the book, by cutting down drastically on the subplots involving Mrs Dubose and Miss Maudie. It was less concerned than the book with tracing the *Bildungsroman* theme of the children growing up in a community through learning to be tolerant.

As the movie prioritized the trial, it made an icon of the County Courthouse in Monroeville, Alabama, the town in which Harper Lee grew up, and which she used as the model for Maycomb in the book. Production and set designers travelled to Monroeville to photograph and measure the interior, including its visitors' gallery above the court, where the 'negroes' were allowed to sit, in order to reproduce it in minute detail on the Universal Studios soundstages. In turn, the town reinforced the centrality of the courthouse, which was nothing like so salient a setting in the novel, by preserving it as a museum dedicated to the book and movie. The spaces both inside and around the old building serve as sets for a play based on the story staged every year.

But so far as icons are concerned, what about Atticus Finch himself – Scout's father and the heroic lawyer who dares, against the scorn, contempt and threats of the Maycomb townspeople, to defend the alleged black rapist? Countless real-life lawyers have attested to his influence on their choice of profession. 'For nearly four decades the name of Atticus Finch has been invoked to defend and inspire lawyers', as Professor Steven Lubet has written. 'Lawyers are greedy. What about Atticus Finch? Lawyers serve only the rich. Not Atticus Finch. Professionalism is a lost ideal. Remember Atticus Finch.'[2]

And so to Atticus's great summing-up speech for the defence. In the book it takes up over three pages. Even in the film script it looms large, proportionately, weighing in at 537 words, every one of them made impressive, even portentous, by Gregory Peck's emphases. He points out that the 'The state has not produced one iota of medical evidence that the crime Tom Robinson is charged with ever took place', but that there is plenty on Mayella Ewell's face to suggest that she had been beaten by 'someone who led exclusively with his left'. Since Atticus has already shown that Bob Ewell is left-handed, and (a bit too convenient, this) that Tom's left arm is paralysed, the strong supposition must be that Mayella's father beat her 'savagely' when he discovered her with Tom.

All this supports Tom's testimony that Mayella had invited him into her house, kissed him, then accused him of rape only after Bob had discovered them together and beat her about the face. But as Atticus knows, the issue here is not what really happened, but Tom's attitude to Mayella. He has testified that he felt sorry for her:

> And so, a quiet, humble, respectable Negro, who has had the unmitigated TEMERITY to feel sorry for a white woman, has had to put his word against TWO white people's! The defendant is not guilty – but somebody in this courtroom is. Now, gentlemen, in this country, our courts are the great levelers. In our courts, all men are created equal. I'm no idealist to believe firmly in the integrity of our courts and of our jury system – that's no ideal to me. That is a living, working reality! Now I am confident that you gentlemen will review, without passion, the evidence that you have heard, come to a decision and restore this man to his family. In the name of GOD, do your duty. In the name of God, believe . . . Tom Robinson.

Here is the Great American Speech all over again: the appeal to be better than we commonly are, by invoking our founding principle that all men are created equal, so that we may confront and resolve our current dissention.[3]

Courtrooms as sites of theatrical confrontation belong more to fiction than to fact, except when, as in Scottsboro, Alabama, in the 1930s, the legal system wanted to set a public example, to assuage the outrage of the white community and flag up a warning to the black. More commonly, although any American accused of a felony has the constitutional right to a trial by jury, few exercise that right. In real life, as opposed to the movies, most 'cop a plea' – take a lesser charge in return for an admission of guilt – and an even greater percentage of civil cases are settled out of court. Only 5 per cent of serious criminal cases are tried before a jury; of civil disputes only 3 per cent come to trial.

The Verdict (dir. Sidney Lumet, 1982) focuses on this choice. Paul Newman as Boston lawyer Frank Galvin has to decide whether to allow his client, a woman who is in a persistent vegetative state because of medical negligence, to take the miserly compensation offered her by the hospital, or to risk a court trial, after which she might end up with nothing.

Before Gavin takes the case, both sides have wanted to settle out of court. The hospital is offering $210,000; the patient's sister and brother-in-law want the money to move to Phoenix, leaving enough behind to maintain the patient in her care home. But the more Galvin finds out about what happened – the patient, about to deliver, being given an anaesthetic, vomiting into her mask and being deprived of air for several minutes, the baby dying – the more he thinks the hospital is getting off lightly. To restore both justice and his reputation, he turns the offer down.

The patient's relatives are furious. Also ranged against Galvin are the trial judge, who does his best to obstruct Frank's line of questioning, and a wealthy law firm headed by Ed Concannon (James Mason at his most silky-sinister), backed up by a massive legal team. To make matters worse, Frank has started dating Laura Fischer (Charlotte Rampling), who, unbeknown to him, is spying for Concannon.

Concannon wants to win at all costs, including that of the wider sense of justice itself. One evening after a long day's work, when Laura questions the morality of this overriding motive, Concannon answers her with the direct opposite of the Great American Speech, a statement of motive that works to emphasize the rightness of what Frank Galvin will later say when he sums up for the prosecution:

> I know how you feel. You don't believe me, but I do know. I'm going to tell you something that I learned when I was your age. I'd prepared a case and old man White said to me, 'How did you do?' And, uh, I said, 'Did my best.' And he said, 'You're not paid to do your best. You're paid to win.' And that's what pays for this office, pays for the pro bono work that we do for the poor, pays for the type of law that you want to practice, pays for my whiskey, pays for your clothes, pays for the leisure we have to sit back and discuss philosophy as we're doing tonight. We're paid to win the case. You finished your marriage. You wanted to come back and practice the law. You wanted to come back to the world. Welcome back.

As the trial gets under way, things go badly for Frank and his client. One expert witness suddenly goes on holiday for three weeks; another turns out to be elderly and black, his testimony easily shredded by Concannon. Dr Towler, the anaesthetist at the delivery and a leading witness for the defence, turns out to be the distinguished author of a standard obstetrics textbook. Nurses in the delivery room seem to have been drilled by the defence, or gone missing altogether.

Finally, Frank traces the most notable absentee, who served as the admitting-room nurse on the night of the medical accident. She is Kaitlin Costello (Lindsay Crouse), now married and living in New York. She tells Frank that the patient had been admitted to the delivery room having eaten a full meal only an hour before being anaesthetized, and that Dr Towler had ordered her to alter the figure '1' to '9' in the box on the form indicating how many hours earlier the patient had eaten.

Since Frank's cross-questioning has already elicited from Dr Towler that anyone administering a general anaesthetic to a patient who had recently eaten would be guilty of criminal negligence, Kaitlin's testimony blows the defence to smithereens:

> After the operation, when that poor girl she went into a coma, Dr Towler called me in. He told me that he'd had five difficult deliveries in a row and he was tired, and he never looked at the admittance form. And he told me to change the form. He told me to change the '1' to a '9', or else – or else he said, he said he'd fire me. He said I'd never work again. Who were these men? Who were these men? I wanted to be a nurse!

Under intense cross-examination by Concannon, Kaitlin reveals that she can prove her allegation, because she had photocopied the original, unaltered form. Concannon immediately cites some precedent or other to have the photocopy disallowed, then moves to have the whole of

Kaitlin's testimony stricken from the record. Judge Hoyle readily agrees.

But the jury has heard her. So Frank can rise to his magisterial closing speech. As part of a film script by David Mamet, it was bound to be good. It is also one of the clearest, most comprehensive statements of the themes in the Great American Speech to be found in the movies:

> You know, so much of the time we're just lost. We say, 'Please, God, tell us what is right; tell us what is true.' And there is no justice: the rich win, the poor are powerless. We become tired of hearing people lie. And after a time, we become dead, a little dead. We think of ourselves as victims, and we become victims. We become – we become weak. We doubt ourselves, we doubt our beliefs. We doubt our institutions. And we doubt the law. But today you are the law. You ARE the law. Not some book, not the lawyers, not the – a marble statue, or the trappings of the court. See those are just symbols of our desire to be just. They are, they are, in fact, a prayer: a fervent and a frightened prayer. In my religion, they say, 'Act as if ye had faith, and faith will be given to you.' IF – if we are to have faith in justice, we need only to believe in ourselves. And ACT with justice. See, I believe there is justice in our hearts.

And it works. The jury not only brings in a verdict of guilty; they even ask if they can increase the damages. The movie succeeded too, garnering great critical praise and five Academy Awards nominations: best actor, best supporting actor, best director, best screenplay from another medium and best picture overall. On a budget of $16 million, it grossed $54 million and netted $26,650,000 on rentals in the U.S.

Galvin's and Finch's summings-up are just two of many Great American Speeches that have lodged in the American public memory and popular culture, not because they square with contemporary reality – what Ed Concannon calls 'the World' – but because they voice the hope of something better.

Yet how the jury responds to the Great American Speech seems to be irrelevant to its reception by the wider audience of the film. After all, Atticus hardly restores justice in *To Kill a Mockingbird*. The jury finds Tom guilty and he is condemned to death. Despite Atticus's assurance that he will appeal to a higher court, Tom tries to escape and is shot to death in the attempt; so he so virtually commits suicide. Bob Ewell continues his vindictive violence against the Finch family, spitting in Atticus's face and finally attacking Jem and Scout one night with a knife, only to be prevented by the mysterious Boo Radley, who turns the knife on Bob himself.

At this point the sheriff and (finally, reluctantly) Atticus, the great model of the disinterested lawyer and champion of justice, decide to agree on the lie that Ewell fell on his own knife and that Boo was the innocent rescuer of Jem and Scout. There may be a higher justice in this collusion, but it has nothing to do with any transformative power liberated by Atticus's concluding speech.

Yet even more than Frank Gavin's, Atticus Finch's summing-up has been remembered as the archetypal

Great American Speech. It stands as another monument, like those shrines in Washington, DC, possibly inspiring and interrogating the imaginations of those passing by, but never working a direct cause-and-effect result on the action going on around them, standing apart as a beacon of the good.

Afterword

Two Discourses

In July 1964, less than a year after the great March on Washington, President Lyndon B. Johnson signed John F. Kennedy's Civil Rights Bill outlawing discrimination on the grounds of race, colour, sex or national origin.

Of course, it took Johnson's vast experience of legislative politics to get the bill through Congress, together with Kennedy's assassination in November 1963, a tragedy Johnson was quite ready to exploit when he told a joint session of Congress that 'No memorial oration or eulogy could more eloquently honor President Kennedy's memory than the earliest possible passage of the civil rights bill for which he fought so long.'

This was a happy example of a unifying event following one of those great calls for unity expressed in the Great American Speech. Unfortunately, it was also a unique example. In other cases events overthrew the sentiment. Jefferson's call for a unified politics was followed by inter-party rivalry even more bitter than before. Lincoln's plea for the power of the Union specifically and 'union' morally was followed by the most extreme negation possible of those values, a Civil War that killed 750,000 Americans.[1]

It might be said that our finer oratorical expressions of communal values run so counter to actual American experience and practice as almost to constitute what Marxists used to call false consciousness. But that would be wrong. Experience challenges the ideal at all times, and everywhere, not just in the United States.

What we are dealing here goes beyond the clash between theory and practice. Our conflict is between two separate discourses of American national identity. One idealizes self-reliance, the other the impulse to share. Both enshrine democracy as Americans' defining value, but they disagree on how that polity is best produced and defended.

So radical is this contradiction between ideals that it sometimes leads to acts of violence with national repercussions. Lincoln was assassinated only five days after the South's surrender guaranteed the Union would survive. Kennedy was murdered just over a month after his partial test-ban treaty came into force. Martin Luther King Jr survived his major rhetorical triumph for five years, but was gunned down on 4 April 1968, after he had begun to campaign for the rights of poor people generally, not just African Americans. Do those public figures who so proclaim the best we stand for always invite an assassin who feels a challenge to his soul?

And do Americans revere and monumentalize their speeches retrospectively for their inherent value and their appeal to their better angels, or out of sorrow, or even remorse?

The Ambassador Hotel

The day after Martin Luther King Jr was shot on the balcony of a Memphis motel, Robert F. Kennedy, now a candidate for president himself, gave the speech of his life. As his venue, he chose the prominent American debating forum of the City Club of Cleveland.

His inescapable theme, the phrase by which the speech has become known, was 'The Mindless Menace of Violence'. His argument was the urgent need – above all in the American 1960s – to renounce violence as a way of settling disputes with, or of expressing fear or suspicion of, our fellow citizens. As befitted an indoor meeting, he spoke quietly, but also slowly, with frequent pauses for emphasis.

Although he began his remarks by saying, 'This is a time of shame and sorrow. It is not a day for politics' (he had announced his candidacy only twenty days earlier), the speech was intensely political. Conventionally enough (though he voiced the sentiment very movingly indeed), he deplored the gun and bomb as a way of expressing disapproval, but he also mentioned other kinds of violence that 'brings retaliation', the violence

of institutions; indifference and inaction and slow decay. This is the violence that afflicts the poor, that poisons relations between men because their skin has different colors. This is a slow destruction of a child by hunger, and schools without books and homes without heat in the winter.

Just two months later Robert F. Kennedy himself fell victim to the harder kind of violence. He had just won the California Democratic primary for the presidency when just after midnight on 5 June a Palestinian militant shot him down in the kitchens of the Ambassador Hotel as he was leaving via a short cut after thanking his supporters in that contest.

So how did the movies deal with this most striking instance of the dialogue between the discourses of competition and cooperation? In the last ten minutes or so of running time in the film *Bobby* (dir. Emilio Estevez, 2006), the mayhem following the shooting is over-voiced by a recording of his speech against the 'Mindless Menace of Violence': 'Too often we honor swagger and bluster and the wielders of force', Kennedy said then and in the movie. 'Too often we excuse those who are willing to build their own lives on the shattered dreams of others.' Violence becomes a way of life, he added, when

> We learn, at the last, to look at our brothers as aliens, men with whom we share a city, but not a community, men bound to us in common dwelling, but not in common effort. We learn to share only a common fear – only a common desire to retreat from each other – only a common impulse to meet disagreement with force.

Within the aesthetic frame of the film, how does this tension work between the violent chaos surrounding the assassination and the ideals being expressed in the voice-over? Among film analysts the received wisdom holds that pictures always come over as 'truer' than words. The classic example of this axiom is the end of *Klute* (dir. Alan J. Pakula, 1971) in which the sophisticated and unromantic New York call girl Bree Daniels (Jane Fonda) is packing to go and live in Tuscarora, Pennsylvania, with John Klute (Donald Sutherland), the out-of-town detective who has investigated a murder case in which she was tangentially involved and (incidentally) stopped her from being killed herself by the obsessional murderer.

In the empty flat, with her things in boxes, as Bree finishes her packing, we hear her talking in a voice-over to her psychiatrist (Vivian Nathan), whom she has consulted from time to time during the movie:

> Bree: I've explained to him what I have to do – and I think he understands. What could ever happen for us? I mean, we're so different. I know enough about myself to know that whatever – lies in store for me it's not going to be – setting up housekeeping with somebody in Tuscarora – and darning socks and doing all that. I'd go out of my mind. It's so hard for me to say it! God!
>
> Vivian: To say what?
>
> Bree: I'm going to miss him.

Though the pictures and the voice-over tell a different story, Colin McCabe has written, the picture wins out. 'The Camera . . . tells the truth, that what Bree really wants to do is to settle down in the mid-West [*sic*] with John Klute.'[2]

If the pictures over-rode the words in *Bobby*, then the movie could be said to end in savage irony, as Kennedy's exalted and reasoned plea against violence is cancelled out by the meaningless violence of his own death and its immediate aftermath. Yet the film came out in 2006, 38 years after the catastrophe – long enough to dull the pain of Bobby's murder, while reinforcing the timeless value of what he had to say following King's assassination. The year 2006 was also when the Democrat fight-back began, in the form of the party's sweeping victories in the mid-term election, capturing both houses of Congress and a majority of governorships and state legislatures.

When asked during the 2008 Democrat primary race if he had been inspired by the example of Kennedy, Barack Obama answered, 'Yes – Bobby Kennedy.' So by then maybe those words had come to outweigh the tragedy even of Bobby's death.

Healing

What Bobby Kennedy's Mindless Menace address also showed is that the American Speech can go beyond its commemorative function to be deployed as an active intervention in contemporary events. Who knows – perhaps its highest calling is to heal the nation's wounds. This happened again on 12 January 2011, when President Obama visited Tucson, Arizona, to deliver a classic memorial speech after a psychopath shot nineteen people at a political meeting, killing six, one of whom was a girl of nine.

In an era of vicious partisanship between communitarians and enterprisers, between public service and small government, Obama warned that 'What we can't do is use this tragedy as one more occasion to turn on each other.'

Instead we need to talk to each other 'in a way that heals, not in a way that wounds'.

Then he turned to the tragedy of the dead girl:

That's what I believe, in part because that's what a child like Christina Taylor Green believed. Imagine: here was a young girl who was just becoming aware of our democracy; just beginning to understand the obligations of citizenship; just starting to glimpse the fact that someday she too might play a part in shaping her nation's future. She had been elected to her student council; she saw public service as something exciting, something hopeful. She was off to meet her congresswoman, someone she was sure was good and important and might be a role model. She saw all this through the eyes of a child, undimmed by the cynicism or vitriol that we adults all too often just take for granted.

Setting his script aside, he added, 'I want America to be as good as she imagined it.'

Even Fox News was moved, temporarily, when an All Star Panel on a Special Report praised the speech that night. The following day it was business as usual, when radio shock jock Rush Limbaugh tore a strip off Fox News for 'slobbering' over Obama's speech: 'They were slobbering over it for the predictable reasons. It was smart, it was articulate, it was oratorical. It was, it was all the things the educated, ruling class wants their members to be and sound like.'

In this, the cynical voice of Jackie Cogan in *Killing Them Softly*, the Great American Speech has emerged, once again, as a class issue. But Obama's point was not to persuade Americans that things were other than they were, just that they should want them to be so. That aspiration has been the theme of the Great American Speech from its inception.

Is it All Over?

But when, four years later on 9 August 2014, an unarmed black teenager called Michael Brown was shot down by a white policeman in Ferguson, Missouri, and when three months after that a grand jury failed to indict the officer involved, the president sidestepped a classic opportunity to remind America of a better way, to strive to be as good as can be imagined. Why? Did he fear that his own colour would make another such appeal seem partisan? Was he too preoccupied with myriad foreign developments overseas – themselves too diverse to allow a single, clear policy response to be formulated in yet another Great American Speech? Are current affairs now simply too complex for that kind of rhetoric?

Meanwhile, with the Great American Speech all but vanished from the movies (though living on in television series like *The West Wing* and *The Newsroom*) and one of its greatest defenders and practitioners fallen silent, it is left for the monuments in stone to stand as our timeless reminders. But watch this space.

References

PART ONE: A COMMON CULTURE

1 'Clinton Sharpens Barbs Against Obama', http://abcnews.go.com, 14 February 2008.

2 '"Don't Tell Me Words Don't Matter!": Obama's Best Speech Yet', 17 February 2008, www.youtube.com.

3 Richard Toye, *The Roar of the Lion: The Untold Story of Churchill's World War II Speeches* (Oxford, 2013).

4 David Reynolds, review of *The Roar of the Lion*, *The Guardian* (16 August 2013).

1 Immigrants and the American Dream

1 For an excellent account of reasons advanced for the western planting, see Klaus E. Knorr, *British Colonial Theories, 1570–1850* (London, 1963), pp. 42–4.

2 John Smith, 'A Description of New England', in *The Complete Works of John Smith (1580–1631)*, ed. Philip L. Barbour (Chapel Hill, NC, 1986), vol. I, pp. 342–3.

3 For a fuller discussion of this process, see Stephen Fender, *Sea Changes: British Emigration and American Literature* (Cambridge, 1992).

4 William Cobbett, *A Year's Residence in the United States of America* (London, 1838), para. 331.

5 Morris Birkbeck, *Notes on a Journey in America from the Coast of Virginia to the Territory of Illinois* (London, 1817), pp. 136–7; 103, 102, 149.

6 Cobbett, *A Year's Residence*, pp. 392–3.

7 Thomas Welde to his former parishioners in Tarling, Essex,

June/July 1632, in Nehemiah Wallington, 'Copies of Profitable and Comfortable Letters', British Library, Sloane MSS 922, f. 92.

8 Thomas and Jane Morris to his father, Washington County, Ohio, early 1832, in *Invisible Immigrants: The Adaptation of English and Scottish Immigrants in Nineteenth-century America*, ed. Charlotte Erickson (London, 1972), p. 155.

9 John Harden to his parents from New York State, in William Cobbett, *The Emigrant's Guide: In Ten Letters Addressed to the Tax-payers of England* (London, 1829), p. 81.

10 Edward Phillips from Greenville Illinois to his father in Shropshire, 1842, in *Invisible Immigrants*, ed. Erickson, p. 271.

11 John Burgess, Westchester County, New York, to Thomas Hallett, Ditchling, Sussex, 1794, East Sussex Records Office, AMS, 5853, in *No Continuing City* [NCC]*: The Diary and Letters of John Burgess, a Sussex Craftsman, Between 1785 and 1829*, ed. Donald F. Burgess (Redhill, 1989), p. 92.

12 Birkbeck, *Notes on a Journey*, p. 8.

13 Cobbett, *A Year's Residence*, paras 427–8; George Rose (1744–1818) served at the Court of Exchequer during the Pitt administration, and was later made vice-president of the Committee on Trade and joint Paymaster General.

14 Cobbett, *The Emigrant's Guide*, pp. 43–4.

15 Smith, 'A Description of New England', vol. 1, p. 344.

2 'City on a Hill': The Communitarian Vision

1 Gabor S. Boritt, *Lincoln and the Economics of the American Dream* (Urbana, IL, 1994) p. 1.

2 'John Dane's Narrative, 1682', *New England Historical and Genealogical Register*, VIII (1834), pp. 154–5.

PART TWO: THE GREAT AMERICAN SPEECH

1 Fred Kaplan, *Lincoln: The Biography of a Writer* (New York, 2008), p. 2.

2 Robert V. Remini, *Andrew Jackson and the Bank War* (New York, 1967), p. 82.

3 Kaplan, *Lincoln*, p. 321.

3 Inaugurals: Adams, Jefferson and America's First Parties

1 Cited in Jeffrey K. Tulis, *The Rhetorical Presidency* (Princeton, NJ, 1987), p. 51.

2 'Publius' [James Madison], 'The Federalist XLIX', in *The Debate on the Constitution*, ed. Bernard Bailyn, Library of America (1993), vol. II, pp. 145–6.

3 Tulis, *The Rhetorical Presidency*, pp. 97, 133, 135–6.

4 Eric Foner, *Give Me Liberty!: An American History* (New York, 2006), pp. 247–8.

5 This was another of Thatcher's speeches ghostwritten by Sir Ronald Millar; it may have suited the occasion, but not the speaker's personality and politics, and therefore hasn't survived like 'the lady's not for turning'.

6 *A Defence of the Constitutions of Government of the United States* (London, 1787).

7 'Publius' [James Madison], 'The Federalist X', in *The Debate on the Constitution*, ed. Bailyn, vol. I, pp. 405, 410–11.

4 Webster and Lincoln: Monuments and Memory

1 Craig R. Smith, *Daniel Webster and the Oratory of Civil Religion* (Columbia, MO, 2005), p. 8.

2 Garry Wills, *Lincoln at Gettysburg* (New York, 1992), p. 27.

3 United States Army, 'The Battle of Gettysburg: Statistics', www.army.mil, accessed 15 August 2014

4 Wills, *Lincoln at Gettysburg*, p. 22.

5 Ibid., pp. 53–9. There are also subsidiary topics within the two main sections, for which see pp. 59–61.

6 Ibid., p. 172.

7 Theodore Parker, 'Transcendentalism', in *The Centennial Edition* [of the Works of Theodore Parker], vol. VI, p. 30; cited in Wills, *Lincoln at Gettysburg*, p. 107.

8 Ibid, p. 132.

9 Eric Foner, *Give Me Liberty!: An American History* (New York, 2006), p. 412.

10 Wills, *Lincoln at Gettysburg*, p. 88.

11 Charles Sumner, *The Promises of the Declaration of Independence: Eulogy on Abraham Lincoln, delivered before the municipal authorities of the city of Boston, June 1, 1865* (Boston, MA, 1865), p. 40.

5 A Common Humanity: Kennedy Confronts the Soviets

1 Robert Schlesinger, *White House Ghosts: Presidents and Their Speechwriters* (New York, 2008), pp. 107–8.
2 Sam Leith, *You Talkin' to Me? Rhetoric from Aristotle to Obama* (London, 2011), p. 267.
3 Schlesinger, *White House Ghosts*, p. 107.
4 The Pentagon Papers, vol. II, chapter 1, 'The Kennedy Commitments', http://media.nara.gov; James K. Galbraith, 'Exit Strategy: In 1963, JFK Ordered a Complete Withdrawal from Vietnam', *Boston Review* (October/November, 2003).
5 Eric Foner, *Give Me Liberty!: An American History* (New York, 2006), p. 853.
6 Schlesinger, *White House Ghosts*, pp. 130–31.
7 Ibid., p. 133.

6 Unity and the Union: Lincoln and Martin Luther King Jr

1 Garry Wills, *Lincoln at Gettysburg* (New York, 1992), p. 130.
2 Ibid., p. 158.
3 Ibid., p. 159.
4 Fred Kaplan, *Lincoln: The Biography of a Writer* (New York, 2008), p. 327.
5 Martin Luther King Jr, *Strength in Love* (Philadelphia, PA, 1963), p. 6.
6 The judgment was handed down as 'Brown v. Board of Education of Topeka, Kansas', 347 U.S. 483 (1954).
7 Gary Younge, *The Speech: The Story Behind Martin Luther King's Dream* (Chicago, IL, 2013), pp. 102–4.
8 Ibid., p. 95.
9 Dolan Hubbard, *The Sermon and the African American Literary Imagination* (Columbia, MO, 1994), p. 8.
10 Lyndrey A. Niles, 'Rhetorical Characteristics of Traditional Black Preaching', *Journal of Black Studies*, 15 (1984), p. 51.

PART THREE: THE MOVIES: THE RISE AND FALL
OF THE MORAL MOMENT

1 See 'Bankers and Common Men in Bedford Falls: How the FBI Determined that *It's a Wonderful Life* Was a Subversive Movie', *Film History*, 10 (1998), p. 314.

2 The clash between Steinbeck the journalist and Steinbeck the novelist is discussed more fully in Stephen Fender, *Nature, Class and New Deal Literature: The Country Poor in the Great Depression* (New York, 2012), pp. 157–78.

7 Six Monuments and a Filibuster: The Other Discourse
of *Mr Smith Goes to Washington*

1 Apparently a nodding toy, hence a brainless puppet; the term seems to have been coined for this film.

8 The Great Trial Scene: *The Verdict* and *To Kill a Mockingbird*

1 Hollace Ransdell, 'Report on the Scottsboro, Alabama Case', http://law2.umkc.edu, accessed 24 June 2014.

2 Steven Lubet, 'Reconstructing Atticus Finch', *Michigan Law Review*, 97 (1999), pp. 1339–62.

3 In racial hatred this time, rather than class divisions, for if anything, Atticus exploits the status of Bob and Mayella as white trash.

Afterword

1 For long the official toll stood at 618,222, but recent work on newly digitalized census data has raised that figure by over 20 per cent. See Guy Gugliotta, 'New Estimate Raises Civil War Death Toll', *New York Times* (2 April 2012).

2 Colin McCabe, 'Realism and the Cinema: Notes on Some Brechtian Theses', *Screen*, 15 (1974), pp. 7–27, 11.

Acknowledgements

My thanks to the journalist Fiona Sandiford, who read three draft chapters, generously offering suggestions that had the effect of ironing out the tangles of my academic prose in favour of a more readable style.

Thanks also to the computer programmer Jennifer Wall, who helped me through a number of difficult searches on the Internet.

Janet Pressley, my former student at the University of Sussex and long-time friend, also helped out with repeated readings and suggestions. But her role was more central, in that she really gave me the idea of the book in the first place, when she asked me if I had noticed that no matter how melodramatic or even violent an American movie, there was often a moment when someone spoke up to reclaim the moral high ground, almost as though they were giving a homily about how we could be better – in particular, how much happier we could be if we could cooperate rather than contend. That got me thinking about more formal American speeches – the ones that Americans remembered, made part of the culture, even turned into monuments – and how surprising it was that instead of championing the virtues of competitive self-reliance that were supposedly at the heart of the country's national identity, these much-loved treasures of oratory argued passionately for equality and cooperation in the spirit of America's founding document, the Declaration of Independence.

Snty-tact, copyright holder of the image on p. 8, has published this online under conditions imposed by a Creative Commons Attribution 3.0 Unported License.

Index